GREAT GARDENS OF
LONDON

To Richard Vine, gardener in the sky

Frances Lincoln Limited
74–77 White Lion Street
London N1 9PF
www.franceslincoln.com

Great Gardens of London
Copyright © Frances Lincoln Limited 2015
Text © Victoria Summerley 2015
All photographs © Marianne Majerus and
Hugo Rittson Thomas 2015, except page 7
top right, Gibbons Rent © Cityscapes;
bottom right, author's garden © Steven Wooster.
Page 8 bottom, garden bridge © ARUP.

First Frances Lincoln edition 2015

A catalogue record for this book is available
from the British Library.

ISBN 978-0-7112-3611-0

Printed and bound in China

1 2 3 4 5 6 7 8 9

GREAT GARDENS OF
LONDON

Text by Victoria Summerley Photographs by Marianne Majerus and Hugo Rittson Thomas

F

FRANCES LINCOLN LIMITED

Photograph by Marianne Majerus

Leucanthemum × superbum
'T.E. Killin', the dark spheres of *Allium
sphaerocephalon* and the grasses
Deschampsia cespitosa 'Goldschleier'
and *Stipa calamagrostis* meld into an
eye-catching display in the Europe
Garden at the Queen Elizabeth
Olympic Park.

INTRODUCTION

Throughout London, you can often catch glimpses of gardens – great, grand and small – from the top of a bus or through the railings as you walk past. *Great Gardens of London* will give you a private view of what is inside, and a chance to meet the people who maintain, restore and design these extraordinary places.

I lived and worked in the capital for thirty years before moving to the Cotswolds, yet driving through Admiralty Arch in a taxi and bowling down The Mall towards Buckingham Palace still gives me a child-like thrill. To me, London has always been the most glamorous city in the world. It has a kind of majesty that impresses even those of us who are familiar with it, thanks to its royal parks – Green Park, St James's, Hyde Park and Kensington Gardens – which provide the landscape equivalent of a roll of drums or fanfare of trumpets. They heighten the impact of landmarks such as Buckingham Palace with a spacious setting, where the visitor can stop to absorb what is around them.

London is a vibrant city that works hard, and its history is put to work too, whether as a home, office and venue for official receptions – as in the case of Buckingham Palace and Clarence House (see page 44) – or as a busy tourist attraction, such as Hampton Court (see page 36) or the Tower of London, which is visited by nearly three million people every year.

For such a sprawling metropolis, London is a surprisingly green city – roughly 45 per cent of Greater London is green space.

Outside the centre, there are abundant parks and commons (originally, common grazing land and still fiercely protected by legislation). Some of these spaces – such as Richmond Park and Greenwich Park – are royal legacies, but the commons bear witness to the fact that London is a network of villages, which over the years have been swallowed up by the ever-expanding city.

Perhaps that village mentality still lurks within the DNA of even the most sophisticated metropolitans, because, as well as the many green spaces, London's gardens offer a huge variety of styles and plants. Like the city's architecture, they are a beguiling mix of old and new.

Residents who do not have their own garden will colonize balconies, windowsills and doorsteps with planters containing anything from evergreen shrubs and pelargoniums to herbs and vegetables. One of the most spectacular interpretations of this theme is the 10m/30ft-long window box outside the restaurant Locanda Locatelli, designed by Declan Buckley and planted as a wildflower meadow.

At Gibbon's Rent, a Cityscapes project which transformed a neglected alleyway in Bermondsey into a community garden, landscape architects Sarah Eberle and Andrew Burns have used concrete sewer pipes as containers. Their size means that they offer a generous planting area, while at the same time matching the scale and style of the surrounding buildings.

The guerrilla gardening movement, led by Richard Reynolds, aims to green up unused space such as roundabouts and grass verges. Reynolds once designed a pop-up garden in a skip, using plant material from show gardens, to publicize his campaign at RHS Hampton Court Palace Flower Show.

A CITY FOR GARDENERS

Fortunately, it is easy to buy plants in London. The street markets may be slowly shrinking, but they are still there, offering trays of bedding plants alongside the fruit and veg. Just as there is usually a park within a couple of streets of where you live, there is very often a garden centre of some description too.

Enthusiastic gardeners can take advantage of the Royal Horticultural Society's shows – not just the blockbusters such as Chelsea and Hampton Court Palace, but also the smaller ones held at the Horticultural Halls near Victoria, which feature anything from spring plants and potatoes to orchids and alpines.

Even the Garden Museum, thought to be the only one of its kind in the world, is based in London, at the former church of St Mary-at-

Lambeth, next door to Lambeth Palace. It organizes three temporary exhibitions each year, and its Knot Garden, inspired by seventeenth-century design, pays tribute to the plant hunter John Tradescant the Elder and his son, also John, who are buried in the churchyard.

Knot gardens are still popular today, as you will see when you turn the pages of this book, but a quick browse through the many hundreds of London gardens which open for the National Gardens Scheme will show you that, for every traditional English-style garden in the capital, there is one that pushes the boundaries either in terms of design or horticulture. The work of some of the UK's best garden designers – such as Dan Pearson, Mary Keen, Christopher Bradley-Hole, Tom Stuart-Smith, Declan Buckley and Bunny Guinness – can be found across the capital.

Contemporary garden design is well-suited to London life, since it can easily incorporate barbecues and pizza ovens for outdoor entertaining, as well as features such as lighting schemes. Innovations are not only design-led, however – London's cosmopolitan population and its warm microclimate mean that all sorts of other influences are at work.

My former garden in Wandsworth, which I opened for charity under the National Gardens Scheme, was a subtropical jungle of hardy bananas, bamboos, tree ferns, palms and cannas, with climbers such as *Campsis grandiflora* and *Trachelospermum jasminoides* enhancing the unusual effect.

Above This Living Wall forms part of the Rubens Hotel, in central London.
Above right Sarah Eberle and Andrew Burns designed Gibbon's Rent.
Below right Victoria Summerley's former garden in Wandsworth, London featured exotic plants such as bananas and cannas.

On London's thriving allotments, the spinach-like leaves of callaloo (*Amaranthus*), a favourite West Indian dish, are now a common sight alongside south-east Asian vegetables such as Vietnamese mustard and yard-long beans. And many gardeners grow chillies and peppers – just ask allotment-holder and prize-winning garden designer Cleve West, himself of Anglo-Indian descent.

Despite the 2008 economic crisis, London remains a comparatively affluent area. New public planting projects, such as the Olympic Park (see page 82), have been not only successful but also inspirational, encouraging gardeners throughout the UK to try to grow their own pictorial meadows.

The latest project, a plan to build a garden bridge across the Thames from Temple to the South Bank, was given planning permission in autumn 2014 by Westminster City Council and Lambeth Council. The multi-million pound pedestrian bridge, planted with grasses, trees and wild flowers, has been designed by Thomas Heatherwick, who also created the cauldron made up of 204 copper torches for the 2012 London Olympics.

Great Gardens of London is aimed at residents and visitors alike, at lovers of both gardens and design, and at those who are curious about London's long and fascinating history. Within these pages, they will find gardens on boats and rooftops as well as in backyards. All are testament to the fact that, wherever there is space to put a pot, Londoners will try to grow a garden.

Top The Green Dock, at the Thames Barrier Park in east London, was opened in 2000; it was created by renowned horticulturists Alain Cousseran and Alain Provost.

Above Thomas Heatherwick's design for a garden bridge across the Thames includes the use of trees and wild flowers.

CHAPTER ONE
POMP AND CIRCUMSTANCE

SEAT OF POWER

10 DOWNING STREET, WESTMINSTER

Some gardens are created great, and some have greatness thrust upon them. In the case of the garden behind 10 Downing Street, the home of British prime ministers since 1735, this pleasant 0.2 hectares/½ acre has been somewhat bypassed by the fashions of landscape architecture. At the same time, it has been a witness to some of the most important events, and some of the most charismatic politicians, in British history.

Ironically, William Kent – the man who had such a huge influence on Britain's great eighteenth-century landscape gardens – was the architect who transformed No. 10 into the residence that we know today. George II had offered the house to Sir Robert Walpole, effectively Britain's first prime minister, in 1732. Walpole said that he would not accept the house as a gift, but suggested that it become the official residence of the First Lord of the Treasury, a title that is now always held by the prime minister.

This sounds very principled and proper, but Walpole, who had nearly bankrupted himself building Houghton Hall, his family seat in Norfolk, was probably horrified at the thought of taking on another expensive building project. By nominating the

house as the residence of the First Lord of the Treasury, it meant that the Treasury had to pay for refurbishments and alterations.

As Kent had previously been commissioned to design the interiors for Houghton Hall in Norfolk, he was a natural choice for Downing Street. It was the interiors that required work, so Kent concentrated on these, rather than the back garden – even though he was the creator of Rousham, one of the best-preserved English Landscape-style gardens. At the time, the Downing Street garden consisted only of a small terrace. A painting – now in the Museum of London – of Walpole standing on this terrace shows that it backed directly on to St James's Park.

AMERICAN INFLUENCE

It is only since the early 1980s, when Downing Street became more of a family home for prime ministers from Margaret Thatcher onwards, that the garden has really been used for domestic and public occasions.

Prime Minister John Major, under siege from rivals for the Conservative leadership in 1995, announced his 'put up or shut up' challenge from the garden, and it was here that Conservative leader David Cameron and Liberal Democrat leader Nick Clegg announced their coalition pact following the 2010 election.

The Downing Street garden is sometimes known as the Rose Garden, which is inaccurate. The White House in

---

Photographs by Hugo Rittson Thomas

Wisteria grows up the steps that lead to the Cabinet Office terrace, where the prime minister sometimes holds informal meetings in summer.

Washington DC has a rose garden, which is a popular place for American presidents to make press announcements, and Tony Blair once staged a Rose-Garden style press conference at Downing Street with President Bill Clinton, which is probably when the idea of a rose garden originated.

More American influence could be detected in 2011 when Prime Minister David Cameron hosted a barbecue in the garden for military personnel, during a state visit to the UK by President Barack Obama and his wife Michelle. Meanwhile, the arrival of the Camerons' young family has prompted the installation of a play area in the garden.

WILDLIFE POND

Today, the Downing Street garden would not win any medals for garden design. It is not an exercise in metropolitan chic, or horticultural bling – the garden designer and historian Sir Roy Strong condemned the play area as 'ghastly' – but despite this (or perhaps because of this) it is in many ways an archetypal British back garden.

It contains the usual elements – roses, a shady area (most London gardens have a shady area, thanks to trees or buildings in close vicinity), a large lawn, various popular subtropical plants such as cordylines, an echium, dahlias and a *Campsis grandiflora* growing up the wall, as well as raised vegetable beds, introduced

by Sarah Brown, wife of Prime Minister Gordon Brown. In one corner stands an ancient London plane (*Platanus × hispanica*), possibly a remnant of the old St James's Park planting, and a box-leaved azara (*Azara microphylla*), which has chocolate-scented flowers in spring.

In this back garden, however, there are crucial differences. The garden, for example, is maintained by staff from the Royal Parks, who also supply the planting. Most of us would go to a garden centre to buy a bird table, but the one at Downing Street was donated by the BBC programme *Blue Peter*, the longest-running children's television show in the world.

The rose beds, which form an avenue at one end of the garden, were commissioned by Margaret Thatcher. They contain British-grown roses from David Austin Roses, as well as one variety called *Rosa* 'Margaret Thatcher'. Rope swags carrying climbing rose varieties line each side of the pathway.

For most British families, the installation of a wildlife pond would necessitate a weekend of hard digging and laying down of butyl liner. Downing Street's pond was built by the

Above The wooden bird table by the pond was given by the BBC children's programme *Blue Peter*.
Right above The woodland border marks the site of the IRA mortar attack.
Right Topiary and formal bedding ensure the garden looks good year-round.

Wildlife Trusts, the organization that helps to protect natural life throughout the UK.

The wildlife, of course, is oblivious to its historic surroundings. The occasional heron flies in from St James's Park to raid the pond, which is also home each year to a pair of ducks, whose ducklings can often be found exploring the steps to the terrace.

WOODLAND GARDEN

Glance up at a house wall of No. 10 and you can see where the bricks were pockmarked by the Provisional IRA mortar bomb attack on 7 February 1991. The plan had been to assassinate the entire Cabinet, which was meeting to discuss the progress of the first Gulf War. Three shells were fired from a van in Horse Guards Avenue, which was 180 metres/200 yards away, with no direct line of sight.

Above The Rose Garden, with its rope swags, was Margaret Thatcher's idea. Lady Thatcher lived at Downings Street from 1979 to 1990.
Centre left Modern shrub roses, bred by David Austin, frame the view.
Left The pond was built by the Wildlife Trusts. A decoy heron stands guard over the goldfish.
Opposite The sculpture on the main lawn is by Barbara Hepworth.

The IRA had carefully worked out the line of trajectory, using the flags on the surrounding buildings, and had marked the point where they needed to park their van in order to get a direct hit. Overnight snow had obscured the mark, and, of the three shells that were fired, two failed to explode and the third exploded in the back garden of No. 10, leaving a crater 1 m/3 ft or more deep. On hearing the shots, the Cabinet dived under the table for cover. As they re-emerged, Prime Minister John Major said, with traditional British sangfroid: 'I think we had better start again, somewhere else.' According to the security services, if the IRA bombs had found their target, the entire Cabinet would have been killed.

The site of the crater is now a Woodland Garden, where cherry trees blossom in spring above a carpet of bulbs and the scented flowers of *Daphne odora* 'Aureomarginata'.

'The site of the IRA bomb crater is now a Woodland Garden, where cherry trees blossom in spring.'

GARLANDS OF WISTERIA

The No. 10 garden is L-shaped, and the terrace looks out over the short section of the L. Double steps, garlanded with wisteria, descend to the garden, while on the terrace itself big lead planters are filled with seasonal bedding. Many manufacturers today produce faux-lead planters in a style called 'Downing Street', which has a raised grid pattern. Those in the No. 10 garden are the real thing: one bears the date 1666 (the year of the Great Fire of London) and the initials 'CR' (Carolus Rex, that is, Charles II).

The long leg of the L is bounded at the far end by the rose beds, and on the north side by two curving beds of herbaceous planting. Between them, the big lawn, with its Barbara Hepworth sculpture, can easily accommodate 200 guests – or 300, if they happen to be small girls, as in the case of the Brownies, who celebrated in 2014 their 100th birthday with a garden party at Downing Street.

This is all very different to how the garden looked and was used even fifty years ago. A photograph of Prime Minister Harold Wilson's Cabinet taken in the No. 10 garden just after his election in 1964, for example, shows a very straightforward, even boring layout of lawn with a meagre border around the edge. Gardens, just like history, move on. As Leon Trotsky once said: 'change alone endures.'

AN AMERICAN IN LONDON

WINFIELD HOUSE, REGENT'S PARK

It was May 2011 and Barack Obama, forty-fourth president of the United States, was making his first state visit to the UK. It was an important occasion by anyone's standards.

After the presidential helicopter had landed on the lawn of the US ambassador's residence in London, the president decided to snatch a couple of minutes to stretch his legs. He had time for only a brief stroll around the 5-hectare/12½-acre grounds of Winfield House, but it was enough to make a good impression on him. As he returned to the house, President Obama remarked: 'If I had known this property was so nice, I would have applied to be ambassador to London rather than president of the United States.'

Like President Obama, most visitors to Winfield House are surprised by how personal it feels, says head gardener Stephen Crisp. This may reflect the fact that it is a private home (albeit on quite a grand scale), but is also probably due to the way the grounds are managed.

Sustainability is hugely important. This is not only because the garden's upkeep is funded by the US taxpayer, but also because the environment is a key factor for both the residents of Winfield House and Crisp and his team. Thus, 99 per cent of all green waste is recycled (about 60 tonnes a year) and even shredded documents go on the compost heap. Around the garden, there are nest boxes, log piles and a meadow area, while the new pond – built only eighteen months ago – already contains newts.

WOOLWORTH MANSION

Winfield House is the second-largest private garden in London, after Buckingham Palace, but it is far less well known. This is partly because of security, of course, and partly because it is not the actual US embassy, but the home of the US ambassador and his family.

It stands in the middle of Regent's Park, and was originally part of an eighteenth-century development designed by John Nash, the architect responsible for most of Regency London. The original Georgian villa was damaged by fire in the 1930s, and subsequently demolished, after it had been bought by Barbara Hutton, the Woolworth's heiress, in 1936. She then built the present Winfield House – named after Woolworth's founder, Frank Winfield Woolworth.

After the Second World War, Hutton sold the mansion to the American government for $1, and it became the ambassador's

---

Photographs by Hugo Rittson Thomas

Mounds of box and lavender break up the straight edges of the path in a modern take on the classic rose garden at Winfield House.

residence in 1955. Since then, some of the most famous names in recent history have walked in the gardens.

Crisp says he has met every American president since Ronald Reagan (1981–1989), all of whom have planted trees in the garden. His choice for Bill Clinton was an Arkansas water oak (*Quercus nigra*). President Clinton was thrilled, saying that of all the official trees he had ever planted this was the most appropriate. Barbara Bush, wife of President George H. Bush, asked for a personal tour, and Prime Minister Margaret Thatcher regularly came to walk there in her later years, taking advantage of the privacy afforded by this unique backyard.

The latest occupant of Winfield House is US Ambassador Matthew Barzun and his wife Brooke, who came from Louisville, Kentucky in 2013.

BLURRING THE BOUNDARIES

Crisp himself has been at Winfield House since 1987. He trained originally with the Royal Horticultural Society at Wisley, then did an internship at Longwood Gardens in Pennsylvania, the former home of Pierre Du Pont, the American industrialist.

When he arrived at Winfield House, the garden was 'a bit of a Sleeping Beauty' and his mission since then has been to bring it up to the standard he wanted. One of his projects has been to blur the boundaries between the garden and the rest of Regent's Park, to take advantage of the borrowed landscape. A parade of Leyland cypress (× *Cuprocyparis leylandii*) in front of the house has been replaced by *Magnolia grandiflora*, and, in 2000, a Vegetable Garden was planted on the site of an old tennis court, an idea encouraged by Rosemary Verey.

The Barzuns are the ninth family for whom Crisp has worked, and he says it can be a sad moment when an ambassador moves on:

> You build a relationship and then you have to start all over again, but the garden does not change much between one administration and another. If a new family arrives and wants to make subtle changes, they can, but the embassy has allowed me to develop it in a way that I feel is appropriate. In any case, the ambassador usually has a million and one things to think about, whereas I only have to worry about the garden.

Left above The white trelliswork not only provides pattern and interest but also echoes the white-painted window frames of the house.
Left A combination of cleome, cosmos and nicotiana provides a riotously informal contrast with the surrounding box hedge.
Above The white-painted trellis theme is picked up by obelisks in the Rose Garden, which perform a supporting role as well as being decorative.

Mrs Barzun has shown interest in the vegetable garden, as, according to Crisp:

She is very interested in organic gardening, healthy eating and getting children involved in gardening, and we have decided we are going to grow more unusual and heirloom varieties. We do not have much space, so what we do grow has to have added value. It is nice for the ambassador to be able to say at dinner: 'Oh, the pink gooseberries are from the garden...'

Crisp is also responsible for plants and floral arrangements in the house, and here he takes his cue from the resident family: 'Mrs Barzun, being from Kentucky, has a style that I would describe as Contemporary Country. She likes a more informal look – flowers that appear as if they have just been picked from the garden.'

CONTEMPORARY APPROACH

It often surprises people when Crisp explains that he and two other gardeners manage the whole 5 hectares/12½ acres. 'It is about having a hierarchy of priorities,' he says. 'The grounds closer to the house require more attention, while the further reaches can be softer and more natural.'

In any case, the emphasis on good environmental practice can often have labour-saving – not to mention cost-saving – benefits. The garden is not irrigated, and Crisp is a passionate adherent of the 'right plant, right place' philosophy. The borders are mulched, and what Crisp describes as a multilayer matrix of tree canopy, shrub understorey and ground cover not only adds to the feeling of seclusion but also provides foraging opportunities for birds and other animals, and keeps down weeds.

Four glasshouses produce between 6,000 and 8,000 plants a year for bedding, flowers for the house and general planting. 'They save a huge amount of money,' observes Crisp.

Left The blocks of colour in the Summer Garden, composed of box cubes and late-summer flowers such as rudbeckia, dahlias and echinacea, were inspired by the work of the American architect Frank Lloyd Wright. **Above** Head gardener Stephen Crisp loves plants that 'die elegantly', such as *Verbena bonariensis*, seen here in the foreground, which maintains its airy structure even when the flowers fade in autumn.

'Margaret Thatcher came here for walks in her later years, taking advantage of the privacy in this unique backyard.'

A contemporary approach to planting does away with labour-intensive bedding and also offers a longer period of interest. The Green Garden, for example, uses only four plants: box (*Buxus*), switch grass (*Panicum virgatum* 'Heavy Metal'), pachysandra and golden male fern (*Dryopteris affinis* 'Cristata').

The Summer Garden, which replaced an ageing Rose Garden, gives value for ten months of the year, says Crisp, rather than six weeks in late spring and early summer. It is probably Crisp's favourite area:

> While I was in the States, I saw a lot of designs by Frank Lloyd Wright and I noted that he often used panels of stained glass, a bit like a Mondrian painting. I thought this rectilinear quality might work in the Summer Garden, and I could use panels of planting in a graphic way.

He chose plants that – as he puts it – 'die elegantly': *Verbena bonariensis*, sedum, echinacea and rudbeckia. The stalks and seed heads of these 'new perennials', popularized by designers such as Piet Oudolf, are not cut down until late winter or early spring, thus providing winter interest. Box and olives (*Olea*), clipped into cubes, add an evergreen architectural element.

One of the most recent innovations, which has proved immensely popular, is the Pictorial Meadow, sown for the first time during the Olympics in 2012:

> We had Michelle Obama here [says Crisp] along with David Beckham, various Olympic athletes and 800 schoolchildren. Naturally, the schoolchildren were only interested in David Beckham and the athletes, and did not notice the garden at all – apart from the Pictorial Meadow. This sort of planting seems to appeal to everyone, right across the age range and across class divides.

Naturally, with presidents and other VIPs coming and going, the activity of helicopters has to be taken into account. 'You could not plant a formal parterre in the middle of the lawn,' observes Crisp, drily, 'it would be slightly in the way.'

Above An American eagle looks out over the lawn from its perch beside the cosmos, which flowers all summer, even in containers.
Right above The neat sculptural forms of blue-green echeverias pick up the stone swags of the pots in which they sit.
Right Crisp's design for the Green Garden uses only box, *Panicum virgatum* 'Heavy Metal', pachysandra and *Dryopteris affinis* 'Cristata'.

TALE OF TWO DYNASTIES

ELTHAM PALACE, GREENWICH

If you stand in the parkland at Eltham Palace, it is easy to imagine that you are in the middle of the countryside, far from the capital. The palace is only 13 kilometres/8 miles from Westminster Abbey in the heart of central London. London kilometres are like dog years as far as the hapless commuter is concerned – they always seem to be seven times longer than ordinary kilometres. Even so, entering the palace grounds is a bit like arriving at a magical gateway: there is a very other-worldly feeling about it.

To walk across the moat on the time-worn bridge and see the willow trees (*Salix*) dangling their leafy fingers above the water is romantic in itself. When you learn that the bridge was built in 1396 by Richard II, king of England from 1377 to 1399, the hairs on the back of your neck start to stand up. If you have just driven through the rather unromantic south-east London suburbs in order to get here, the contrast is almost comical.

The palace has an intriguing history. It first came to prominence as a royal residence in the Middle Ages, when English kings enjoyed absolute rule. Eltham Palace was given

Photographs by Hugo Rittson Thomas

This view of the 1930s facade of Eltham Palace, once a Tudor residence and now an Art Deco showpiece, is taken from the wisteria-clad pergola.

to the future Edward II by Anthony Bek, Bishop of Durham, but Edward did not take over the property until after Bek's death in 1311. The Great Hall was built in the 1470s by Edward IV (brother of Richard III, and father of the princes in the Tower). All but the Great Hall was reduced to ruins during the English Civil War. In the first half of the twentieth century, Eltham Palace enjoyed a renaissance, thanks to the heirs of a new kind of dynasty – the textile giant Courtaulds.

ARCHITECTURAL CONTROVERSY

There have always been gardens at Eltham. According to English Heritage, who restored the building in 1999 and opened it to the public, a new garden was laid out in 1384 for Richard II and his wife, Anne of Bohemia. Henry VIII, who grew up at Eltham and who was the last monarch to spend much time there, had a path built from his private apartments to his garden. There was a high fence along the palace side so that he could walk there in privacy.

However, it was the contribution of Stephen Courtauld and his wife Virginia, known as Ginie, that shaped the gardens as you see them today. The couple acquired the lease of Eltham Palace in 1933 and moved in on 25 March 1936. They remodelled the house, retaining whatever historical architecture remained, and redesigned the gardens in the style of the times. This meant building a rock garden beside the moat, installing a sunken

rose garden and creating garden 'rooms', bordered by shrubs, which had been made fashionable by the gardens at Hidcote, Sissinghurst and Great Dixter.

The remodelling was controversial. The architects, Seely and Paget, based their design for the house on Sir Christopher Wren's facade for Hampton Court. At that time, it was thought that Wren had restored the original Tudor palace rather than built a completely new Baroque frontage, so the plan for Eltham was of brick and stone, with tall square chimneys and arched windows. One critic said at the time: 'The other day I found myself confronted with what at first I took to be an admirably designed but unfortunately sited cigarette factory.'

The house has a strangely municipal look. Although its Art Deco interiors are stunning, they are redolent of an era in which luxury was represented by expensive cruises and smart hotels. They have none of the higgledy-piggledy, faded-chintz allure of the average English country house, despite the fact that the Courtaulds had three large dogs and a ring-tailed lemur called Mah-Jongg.

Since 1995, English Heritage has been restoring the house and the gardens as far as possible to the 1930s design. It may seem odd to focus on a tenure that lasted such a short time, but English Heritage are keen to make the most of what they describe as one of the finest examples of a 1930s house

and garden in the UK. The Rose Garden, therefore, is presented as a 1930s Rose Garden, planted with varieties that would have been around at that time, such as *Rosa* 'Gruss an Aachen' (introduced in 1909), *R.* 'Prosperity' (1919), *R.* 'Penelope' (1924) and *R.* 'Felicia' (1926), all hybrid musks.

Christopher Weddell, senior gardens adviser to English Heritage, explained:

Each bed in the Rose Garden has a particular colour scheme – all in paler colours such as peach, pink and pale yellow. We've based these on cinefilm from the Courtaulds' own archive, which shows some of the colours, unlike photographs in, say, *Country Life*, which would have been in black and white.

Virginia Courtauld was the rose enthusiast. She loved roses and irises, whereas Stephen Courtauld loved orchids and alpines. We have some of the varieties that they would probably have bought from breeders like Samuel McGredy, but we don't have a list of every variety they planted.

The old-fashioned rose bed or garden, full of hybrid teas and floribundas that require skilled pruning, was once a staple of any garden, public or private, but it is disappearing fast.

Opposite The wooden bridge across what used to be the south moat was designed by the architects Seely and Paget, who remodelled the house.
Top The fourteenth-century bridge, built by Richard II, originally had a drawbridge at one end.
Above The rock garden was where Stephen Courtauld, an alpine enthusiast, took favoured guests to see his collection.
Right The moat wall, and the hipped roof and high chimney of the 1930s building above it, give the impression of a medieval stronghold.

Top The herbaceous border was designed by Isabelle van Groeningen and has a long season of interest, with crocosmia and miscanthus picking up the baton in late summer.

Left By early summer, the misty blues and soft textures of catmint and hardy geraniums predominate.

Above Spring colour is provided by vivid purple irises and alliums.

Opposite Each bed in the Rose Garden, seen here from the moat wall, has its own colour theme, mainly pastel hues such as pink, pale yellow and apricot.

'Henry VIII, who grew up at Eltham, had a path built from his private apartments to the garden.'

With its soft colours, formal lily pond, low brick wall and lavender hedge, the version at Eltham has a subtle vintage charm.

It also forms part of a wonderful vista that runs from the clipped yew (*Taxus*) in the south moat, through the garden's 'rooms', to the formal pool that now terminates the northern end of the moat.

The garden 'rooms' are not fully enclosed by hedges in the usual Arts and Crafts manner, but formed of open grass courtyards planted on three sides with shrub borders consisting mainly of flowering species such as daphne, osmanthus, viburnum, deutzias, hydrangeas and tree peonies (*Paeonia lutea*).

Trees seem to do well at Eltham Palace. In the South Garden, there are spectacular specimens of *Catalpa bignonioides*, *Liriodendron tulipifera* and *Juglans regia*. Across the moat, in the park, there are giant oaks (*Quercus*), chestnuts – both horse chestnut (*Aesculus hippocastanum*) and sweet chestnut (*Castanea sativa*) – as well as beeches (*Fagus*), while a magnificent sycamore

(*Acer pseudoplatanus*) stretches out one enormous branch as if to compete with the timber bridge.

Below the timber bridge, along the south moat wall, is an herbaceous border designed by Isabelle van Groeningen and planted in 2000 on the site of an existing border. She has used miscanthus, veronicastrum and eupatorium to provide height that is in proportion with the massive brick walls, with sedums, hardy geraniums and catmints (*Nepeta*) at a lower level. In late summer, echinacea, rudbeckia, helenium and helianthus provide brilliant colour, and the planting takes the form of a series of vignettes, with the same plants repeated along the border. This repetition is not obvious, but it gives a subtle sense of coherence.

Restoration of the rock garden above the eastern section of the moat began in 2014. The Japanese maple (*Acer palmatum*) that veils the top of the waterfall, a pine (*Pinus*) and a juniper (*Juniperus*) remain from the original 1938 design, built of Westmorland limestone arranged to replicate the natural strata.

On the opposite side of the moat, magnolias and *Azara microphylla* grow along the wall, below a wisteria-covered loggia whose Ionic columns were salvaged from the Bank of England in the 1930s. It is quite possible to imagine elegant couples sitting beneath the loggia, with their cocktails and 1930s evening attire. Over in the park, however, you can almost hear the faint, mournful note of a Tudor hunting horn.

A GOTHIC FANTASY

STRAWBERRY HILL, TWICKENHAM

Strawberry Hill, like many of the gardens in this book, is the product of one man's vision. Unfortunately, he had that vision quite a long time ago, in 1747, and since then the inexorable advance of London suburbanization has engulfed the countryside, which formerly surrounded this Twickenham mansion.

When Horace Walpole – essayist, author, collector and the son of Britain's first Whig prime minister – first saw Strawberry Hill he was entranced. He decided to remodel what had been a pair of fairly ordinary cottages into a new style, inspired by his fascination with Gothic architecture, and what he called 'the gloomth of [medieval] abbeys and cathedrals'. Thus the first Gothic Revival building came into being.

Walpole was not only the son of a prime minister but also a Member of Parliament, albeit for a rotten borough. (Rotten boroughs were usually controlled by landowners, who gave the 'seat' to friends or relatives. They were finally outlawed in the Reform Act of 1832.)

Walpole's Whig beliefs informed his views on architecture and landscape: he disapproved of what he called the 'absurd

magnificence' of Italian and French villas, and he praised the English Landscape garden style of William Kent who, as Walpole put it, 'leapt the fence and saw that all nature was a garden'.

Strawberry Hill may have been inspired by deeply felt political and aesthetic conviction, but its Gothic character was only skin-deep. Much of the interior decoration, which imitated the fan vaulting and intricate stone carving of medieval cathedrals, was done in wood, or even papier mâché. The carved pinnacles on the roof are of oak, not stone, hidden beneath the 'wedding cake' white paint that conveniently unifies the exterior.

Walpole loved the idea of castles haunted by armoured spectres and paintings that came to life – his *Castle of Otranto*, regarded as the first Gothic novel, was inspired by a nightmare in which a giant mailed fist appeared at the top of the stairs at Strawberry Hill. However, this obsession with romantic melancholy was to have no place in the garden. When a friend, Horace Mann, enquired whether the garden was to be Gothic too, Walpole replied that 'on the contrary, [it] is to be nothing but riant, and the gaiety of nature'.

VIEWS OF THE THAMES
Walpole had strong views on most things, and gardening was no exception. In his essay on landscape design, entitled 'On Modern Gardening', written in 1770, he championed the naturalistic

---

Photographs by Hugo Rittson Thomas

White lilac blossom frames a view of Strawberry Hill. The white-painted walls and the ornate decoration look like some fantastical wedding cake.

style of William Kent and Charles Bridgeman (who designed the parklands of his father's house at Houghton Hall in Norfolk) and commented: 'It is almost comic to set aside a quarter of one's garden to be melancholy in.'

At Strawberry Hill, he wanted to achieve an informal, pastoral effect, with views of the river Thames and the surrounding countryside. In 1753, Walpole wrote this description of the view from his window:

You can see a field which is bounded by a serpentine wood of all kinds of trees and flowering shrubs and flowers. The lawn before the house is situated on the top of a small hill from where to the left you see the town and church of Twickenham . . . and a natural terrace on the brow of my hill, with meadows of my own down to the river, commands both extremities.

Today, the meadows and the view of the river have gone, swallowed up by twentieth-century housing developments.

Walpole died in 1797, leaving the Strawberry Hill estate to his ward, Anne Damer. She could not afford the upkeep of the house, and from her it passed eventually to Frances, Lady Waldegrave, who decided to restore the house in 1856. For twenty years, Strawberry Hill was famous again, partly

as an architectural curiosity and partly as a political salon (Lady Waldegrave, like Walpole, was a Whig).

During the twentieth century, Strawberry Hill fell into disrepair once again. In 2010, thanks to a £9 million restoration by the Strawberry Hill Trust, the house reopened to the public. The garden is open too, but is currently being restored – as far as possible – to its original eighteenth-century design.

THEATRICAL BORDER

The Lime Grove, which Walpole loved, has been replanted, while a replica of his Shell Bench is positioned to give a view of the house. Work has begun on a Theatrical Border, under the expert guidance of garden historian Mark Laird, senior lecturer in landscape architectural history at the Harvard Graduate School of Design, and author of *The Flowering of the Landscape Garden*.

His sketch for the Theatrical Border – a fashion that originated in Paris in the middle of the eighteenth century –

Above Walpole wanted to achieve an informal, pastoral effect at Strawberry Hill, with views of fields and woods.
Right above and **right** The Lime Grove has been replanted to look as it did in Walpole's time, while the Shell Bench, designed by Walpole, is positioned to give a good view of the trees.

Top A Community Garden provides somewhere for local people to grow herbs and other culinary delights.
Above Bluebells flourish along the edge of the woodland.
Left Hellebores are a subtle highlight in the Prior's Garden.
Opposite Walpole built the Gothic screen for the Prior's Garden, which is planted with low box hedges and perennials.

shows a wooded backdrop of small trees and a border of mainly scented shrubs and annuals. Between the two is a trellis fence, and at regular intervals there are specimen plants in striped tubs. The effect is formal without being pompous.

Part of the garden restoration, such as the new lawns, the Prior's Garden (with its Gothic screen) and the Lime Grove, has been financed by the Heritage Lottery Fund, but the money only goes so far. Therefore, head gardener Jennifer Sarginson is reliant on volunteers to help maintain the grounds. She appears to relish the challenge and feels that the small staff at Strawberry Hill, and the Trust's efforts to find new ways of encouraging visitors, make her work more enjoyable rather than less so.

She says that events such as woodland walks and bug hunts during Halloween and the half-term holidays develop a real sense of connection with the local community. In one area of the garden, a woodland storytelling glade has been created, with painted mushroom stools for the children and an ornate carved chair for the storyteller.

Horace Walpole:
'We have given the true model of gardening to the world.'

A Community Garden in front of the wing built by Lady Waldegrave is used by around fifteen local people to grow herbs and vegetables. Many of these now join the volunteers who come in one day a week to help Sarginson and her apprentice.

'We have a huge range of groups visiting Strawberry Hill,' she explains, 'including one group of excluded teenagers who seemed to really love it here. If we do events at Halloween or Easter, they are quickly booked up.'

Obviously, in an ideal world she would like unlimited resources, but in the meantime she is grateful for the support she gets from Painshill Park, the eighteenth-century landscape garden near Cobham, Surrey, which was created by Charles Hamilton between 1738 and 1773. The two gardens have a members' partnership, and a team from Painshill comes to Strawberry Hill every six weeks to lend expertise.

Sarginson is proud of what she has managed to achieve in her time at Twickenham. She would no doubt agree with Horace Walpole's words from his essay 'On Modern Gardening':

We have given the true model of gardening to the world; let other countries mimic or corrupt our taste; but let it reign here on its verdant throne, original by its elegant simplicity, and proud of no other art than that of softening nature's harshness and copying her graceful touch.

JEWEL IN THE CROWN

HAMPTON COURT, EAST MOLESEY

The gargantuan figure of Henry VIII exercises such a fascination for anyone remotely interested in English history that he tends to overshadow other monarchs. Nowhere can this be seen more clearly than at Hampton Court Palace, sited on the river Thames.

Many of the thousands of visitors to the palace each year can tell you about Henry's six wives, and about the legend that the ghost of one of them – Catherine Howard – runs screaming down the Haunted Gallery. Moreover, these visitors may well have lost themselves in the famous Maze, or admired the Baroque facades that look out over the gardens on the south and east sides of the palace, yet they will probably struggle to tell you who commissioned them to be built.

Hampton Court is a palace of two halves. Its Tudor origins can be seen in the ornate chimneys and imposing gateways as you approach the palace from the west. To the east, the Baroque facade designed by Sir Christopher Wren and Nicholas Hawksmoor for William III looks out over the Long Water and the formal gardens originally laid out in the style of André

Le Nôtre, landscape architect to King Louis XIV of France and designer of the gardens at Versailles. To the south is the Privy (or private) Garden, laid out for William III, and restored to its original 1702 design in 1995. From a landscape point of view, there is very little left of the Tudor era, while the seventeenth-century alterations dominate.

PALACE AND PRISON

Who then were the people who left their mark on the palace and the gardens that surround it? Hampton Court was built by Cardinal Thomas Wolsey. He was the son of an Ipswich landowner and had been appointed royal chaplain by Henry VIII's father, Henry VII. When the young Henry VIII ascended the throne in 1509, he found Wolsey to be hardworking, loyal and – crucially – less conservative than the advisers he had inherited from his more cautious father.

For fifteen years, Wolsey was one of the most powerful people in England. His downfall came when he was unable to persuade the Pope to grant Henry VIII a divorce from Catherine of Aragon, so that the king could marry Anne Boleyn. In 1528, Wolsey gave Hampton Court Palace to Henry, in an attempt to placate him. It did not work. Two years later, Wolsey died while travelling from York to London, where he had been summoned to answer charges of treason.

Photographs by Hugo Rittson Thomas

In 1995 the Privy Garden was restored to its original 1702 design. It features plants that would have been known at the time of William III.

Thus Hampton Court became a royal palace, serving not only the Tudors but also the Stuarts, who succeeded them. James I and VI held the Hampton Court conference here, which resulted in the commissioning of a new translation of the Bible.

For his son Charles I, Hampton Court was both palace and prison. He collected many artworks for the palace, among them *The Triumphs of Caesar* by Andrea Mantegna, but he himself was held captive there in 1647, during the English Civil War.

Charles II, who was restored to the throne in 1660, added the canal known as the Long Water, and planted the avenues of lime trees either side. The Wilderness, the area that contains the Maze, was also his innovation and originally contained four mazes.

It was not until 1689, with the accession of William III and Queen Mary to the English throne, that Hampton Court became a favourite royal summer residence once again. The couple were keen gardeners, and one of the first alterations to the garden was the construction of glasshouses to accommodate Queen Mary's 'Exoticks', her world-class collection of plants, which she had brought with her from the Netherlands. The most important change from this era was, however, the rebuilding of the east front of the palace, and the laying out of the Great Fountain Garden and the Broad Walk.

Queen Anne, the sister of Queen Mary, refurbished the Great Fountain Garden in 1707, adding topiary yews that have now grown into the huge mushroom shapes so familiar to visitors today.

HISTORICAL ACCURACY

Despite these changes, the palace remains stubbornly Tudor in the public imagination, and this is something that has exercised those involved in the gardens at Hampton Court for some hundred years.

The palace and its grounds were opened to the public by Queen Victoria, and proved instantly popular with Londoners. In the 1920s, the fashion for all things Tudor led to the creation of the Elizabethan Knot Garden in 1925 and the replanting of Henry VIII's Pond Garden, originally a series of carp ponds providing fish for the palace. These gardens, while popular, were not faithful historical restorations – they were merely fanciful recreations, possibly inspired by the endless requests from visitors to see the 'Tudor gardens' or the 'medieval gardens'.

The same requests come thick and fast today, but the creation in 2009 of a special Tudor Garden in the Chapel Court by

Above These yews were once part of the topiary design in the Great Fountain Garden.
Right above The hornbeam bower, planted in 1995, is the fourth bower since the 1690s to grace the Privy Garden.
Right below Clipped yews and hollies adorn the Privy Garden.

'The newly restored Kitchen Garden has provided another interesting historical insight.'

landscape architect and garden historian Todd Longstaffe-Gowan is based on actual historical research. It uses only plants available in sixteenth-century England, and it is based on the painting *The Family of King Henry VIII*, which hangs in the Hampton Court Palace. In the background of this picture, painted *c.*1545 by an unknown artist, are glimpses of a courtyard in which stand the 'Kyngs beestes' – heraldic emblems such as the golden lion of England, a bull, a dragon, a falcon, a leopard, a greyhound and a white hind or deer, mounted on poles painted in green and white. The same green-and-white poles form a low boundary around Longstaffe-Gowan's design.

The Chapel Court faithfully recreates this image, with herbs and roses planted in the middle two sections, and two areas of lawn at either end. The lawn is a puzzle to some visitors – why, they ask, is it full of weeds, and why is it not neatly mowed? The answer is very simple: they did not have lawnmowers or glyphosate in Tudor times.

Opposite above The Pond Garden originally housed Henry VIII's fishponds, which would have supplied carp for the royal kitchens.
Opposite left The south facade overlooks the Privy Garden.
Top An herbaceous border runs the full length of the Broad Walk, on the east side of Hampton Court Palace.
Above This collection of plants is known as Queen Mary's Exoticks.
Right The Little Pond Garden has a greener, more naturalistic feel.

KITCHEN GARDEN

From 1841 to the 1930s, the Kitchen Garden was rented out to market gardeners, so it has always been in use to some extent. However, the popularity of the grow-your-own movement and the greater interest today in social history – what people ate, how they lived and so on – mean that the newly restored Kitchen Garden is a valuable addition to Hampton Court. It both enhances the overall experience for visitors and provides yet another interesting historical insight. For it, designer Todd Longstaffe-Gowan used John Rocque's Kitchen Garden plan from 1736, although it had been first built for William and Mary in 1689. The Kitchen Garden reopened in mid-spring 2014.

A large information board lists the fruit and vegetables that would have been planted here at the time Rocque drew up his plan. There are sixty varieties of peaches and nectarines – a huge selection compared to those available now. Among all the names and varieties, however, there is no mention of apples – surely one of the most English of fruits. Apparently, apples were the food of the common people. And this is a royal palace, after all.

Above Lawns have replaced the ornate Great Fountain Garden.
Centre left and **left** The Great Vine, thought to be the oldest living vine in the world, produces about 1,000 bunches of grapes per year.
Right The new Kitchen Garden was opened in 2014.

A PRINCE'S PARADISE

CLARENCE HOUSE, WESTMINSTER

At one end of the garden at Clarence House, there is a pair of gates, painted in a smart British racing green. The gates are hung between two brick piers, which are guarded by two stone heraldic lions, seated – or sejant, as the heraldry term has it – beneath the distinctive badge of the Prince of Wales, with its three ostrich feathers rising from a coronet. The gates lead to the compost areas, where neat bins of sweet-smelling crumbly compost are gently rotting down. They are just one of the many reminders in this garden that HRH The Prince of Wales takes his horticulture very seriously.

HISTORIC ROYAL RESIDENCE

Clarence House was originally designed *c*.1825, by the great Regency architect John Nash, for the Duke of Clarence, later William IV. It has always been a royal residence of some kind: the present queen and her husband, Prince Philip, lived at Clarence House before her accession to the throne in 1952, and Princess Anne, Prince Charles's sister, was born there. From 1953, it was the home of Queen Elizabeth the Queen

Mother until her death in 2002. Prince Charles – who was four when he became the heir to the throne – always had a very close relationship with his grandmother, who was a constant reassuring presence when his mother, the queen, was away on State visits abroad.

Her – and now his – garden consists of 0.2 hectares/½ acre, a rectangle that runs parallel with The Mall and is hidden from public view by a wall and a thick holly hedge. A broad path or terrace, lined with lead planters bearing the initial C – a birthday present to Prince Charles – extends the length of the house, which faces south.

A large lawn is dominated by enormous London planes (*Platanus* × *hispanica*) and magnolias, while the occasional specimen tree elsewhere in the garden bears closer examination: one is *Liriodendron chinense*, which came from Highgrove, the Prince's Cotswolds estate, and another is *Magnolia* 'Spectrum', planted by the Dalai Lama in May 2008.

To the right, as you enter the garden, is a box (*Buxus*) parterre, laid out as a cross with a rose at its centre – the symbol of Rosicrucianism. Rosicrucians belong to a kind of philosophical freemasonry with Christian roots, which asserts that ancient wisdom holds the key to the nature of the physical and the divine. One interpretation is that the rose cross symbolizes the body (the cross) and the flowering of the inner consciousness (the rose).

Photographs by Hugo Rittson Thomas

The Prince of Wales created the Rosicrucian parterre, which contains lavender and clipped holm oak (*Quercus ilex*) within box hedges.

SUMMER BEDDING

Mark Lane, gardens manager at Buckingham Palace, whose responsibilities include Clarence House, explains that in the Queen Mother's time the lawn was more extensive and that there was a border of summer bedding, punctuated by standard fuchsias, where the parterre is now planted.

Fashion, in gardens as in dress, is a funny thing. The colourful summer bedding beloved of all our grandmothers was a descendant of carpet bedding, a Victorian innovation. This became possible thanks to the introduction of genera such as petunia and pelargonium, from South America and southern Africa respectively, and the lifting of tax on glass, which made greenhouses much more affordable.

The box parterre, on the other hand, with its roses, salvias and lavender (*Lavandula*), dates back much further, to the seventeenth century and earlier, and includes plants that have been grown in the UK for centuries. Yet the parterre today looks so much more modern than a bed of pelargoniums and petunias that it does not take a Sherlock Holmes to work out that the parterre at Clarence House is the brainchild of the Prince of Wales.

His influence can also be seen in the herbaceous border, which runs nearly the entire length of the garden on the north side. The colour palette chosen by His Royal Highness is of pink, white, mauve and blue.

The border is divided by yew (*Taxus*) buttresses, with a curve at the front of each section of border, which gives a very generous, expansive impression. In some gardens, wooden templates are used to trim hedges such as these, but at Clarence House, explains Mark Lane, a system of colour-coded bamboo canes is employed to ensure that each buttress is identical to its neighbour.

The border itself is not the stiff, staked showcase beloved of the Edwardians but has a more relaxed feel. Pea sticks are used to stop taller perennials flopping too much, while the overall effect is of a country garden, with buddleja and roses giving height alongside perennials such as *Eupatorium purpureum*, *Verbena bonariensis* and Japanese anemones (*Anemone* × *hybrida*). Lower-growing plants towards the front of the border include hardy geraniums, astrantias and *Origanum laevigatum* 'Herrenhausen', and heucheras – *H. villosa* 'Palace Purple' and *H.* 'Prince'. Naturally. The hostas (the Prince has the National Collection of Large-leaved Hostas at Highgrove) and delphiniums are sprayed with garlic to deter slugs, because of course this garden is organic – certified as such by the Soil Association.

Above Claret-red pelargoniums are grown on the balcony above the entrance to Clarence House. The portico roof is used regularly by their Royal Highnesses.

Top and **above** The symbol of Rosicrucianism is the Rosy Cross.
Here the cross is represented by the paths that divide the four sections of
the parterre, and the rose by a flower-shaped box topiary at the centre.
Right A bust commemorates the late Queen Elizabeth the Queen Mother.

Beneath the huge plane trees on the lawn are colonies of wild flowers, including common spotted orchid (*Dactylorhiza fuchsii*) and pyramidal orchid (*Anacamptis pyramidalis*), with its clusters of tiny, bright pink flowers like conical bunches of miniature primulas. The latter are relatively common in the Cotswolds, as they like chalk and limestone grasslands, so perhaps they hitched a lift with some of the plants from Highgrove.

HANDKERCHIEF TREE

One of the first things His Royal Highness installed was the Vegetable Garden, where there is a 'no dig' policy. The theory behind this is that digging destroys the structure of the soil and the balance of the beneficial organisms that live in it. Instead, organic matter such as compost is added in the form of a mulch, and it is taken down into the soil by the action of earthworms.

Top Informal planting in the herbaceous border, which is punctuated by yew buttresses, includes *Macleaya cordata* and agapanthus.
Centre left The Vegetable Garden is run on organic principles.
Far left The bug 'hotel' provides a sheltered habitat for invertebrates.
Left A plaque marks the *Magnolia* Black Tulip planted by Aung San Suu Kyi, leader of the Burmese opposition.
Opposite The stone lions, which crouch at the base of the steps, originally came from the Commonwealth Institute in Kensington.

The vegetables are grown for the kitchen, so the garden staff liaise with the chefs as to what is wanted, and when, because Prince Charles and his wife, the Duchess of Cornwall, are not always in residence. The plot has already expanded from 8 m × 8 m/26 ft × 26 ft to 8 m × 16 m/26 ft × 52 ft, and succession sowing every three weeks ensures a constant supply of produce.

Behind the vegetable bed is a handkerchief tree (*Davidia involucrata*), planted by the Queen Mother. Her herb bed at the eastern end of Clarence House includes an enormous lemon verbena (*Aloysia citrodora*), the size of a buddleja. It is protected by the south-facing wall of the house, so, although its deliciously scented leaves shrivel with the first hard frost, the shrub itself shrugs off the winter cold. The wood is hardy to -10°C/14°F. Fortunately, temperatures that low are unusual in central London.

On summer afternoons, the Queen Mother liked to have tea in the shade of her beloved London planes, the branches of which were allowed to sweep down to the ground. Prince Charles adheres to the same policy of leaving the branches long, in contrast to Buckingham Palace, where the trees are trimmed, says Mark Lane, so as not to discommode garden-party guests. The regulation length should allow clearance for 'a tall gentleman with a top hat'.

That is not to say there are no parties at Clarence House. It is a working palace, and receptions held there often spill out

'Yet more pots contain cornflowers, which Princes Charles likes to wear in his buttonhole.'

into the garden if the weather is good. Yet the ambience remains that of a private garden, possibly because there are so many personal touches.

Tomatoes grow in pots on the sunny terrace, and there are butternut squash on the edge of one of the borders. In the small Rose Garden at the eastern end, there are two beehives, and yet more pots contain cornflowers (*Centaurea cyanus*), which Prince Charles likes to put in his buttonhole.

Various pieces of statuary have been 'recycled', such as the two stone lions that guard the steps to the herbaceous border. They came from the Commonwealth Institute. Some have even been 'upcycled', such as the former stone fountain from Windsor, which is now planted with blue wisteria (to resemble water) and white wisteria (to symbolize the foam of the fountain).

Upcycled, water wise and full of plants – you cannot get much greener than that.

THE LAWS OF HORTICULTURE

INNER TEMPLE, WESTMINSTER

And here I prophesy: this brawl to-day,
Grown to this faction in the Temple-garden,
Shall send between the red rose and the white
A thousand souls to death and deadly night.

This speech by Richard Neville, Earl of Warwick, in Act II, Scene IV of Shakespeare's *Henry VI, Part I*, is like an ominous roll of drums that heralds the beginning of the Wars of the Roses, which finally broke out into armed battle in 1455. In the scene, set according to Shakespeare's own stage directions in 'London, the Temple-garden', Richard Plantagenet, the 3rd Duke of York (great-grandson of Edward III of England and father of Edward IV and Richard III) throws down a challenge to his deadly rival, Edmund Beaufort, Duke of Somerset (grandson of John of Gaunt and head of the House of Lancaster). Plantagenet asks all those present to pick a white rose if they support him, declaring:

Let him that is a true-born gentleman
And stands upon the honour of his birth,

Photographs by Marianne Majerus

Persicaria orientalis drapes itself elegantly along the High Border against a background of rudbeckia and *Amicia zygomeris*.

If he suppose that I have pleaded truth,
From off this brier pluck a white rose with me.

Somerset responds immediately by picking a red rose, and the other noblemen with them choose sides in what was to be a dynastic struggle that lasted for most of the second half of the fifteenth century.

Whether the scene actually occurred in real life is doubtful. The red rose did not become the Lancastrian emblem until 1485. However, there is still a Wars of the Roses border in the garden at Inner Temple, and the white rose of York and the red rose of Lancaster continue to pose problems for the head gardener. The battle, however, is to reconcile the different growth habits of the roses themselves. The white rose – *Rosa alba* – grows to 2.5 m/8 ft, while the red – *Rosa gallica* var. *officinalis* – is much smaller, about 1 m/3 ft high.

Andrea Brunsendorf, head gardener at Inner Temple since 2007, gets around this problem by treating the roses as a sort of basso ostinato, and putting the emphasis on the seasonal planting, using purple and silver to represent red and white. It is very dramatic, but, just as Plantagenet and Somerset's quarrel is a curtain-raiser for a half century of bitter conflict, the Wars of the Roses border plays a secondary role to the most spectacular element in the garden: the High Border.

EXUBERANT PLANTING

There have been gardens at the Temple since the Knights Templar first came to the site, on what is now the Victoria Embankment, in the twelfth century. An inventory dated 1307–1308 shows that a gardener lived on the site, and another, dated 1337, records the sale of fruit from the garden.

In more recent times, Joseph Jekyll, grandfather of Gertrude Jekyll, was superintendent of Inner Temple gardens 1810–1819, while the Royal Horticultural Society (RHS) held its spring show there from 1888 to 1911. The show became so popular that the RHS was forced to move it to the Royal Hospital in Chelsea, to become what we now know as the Chelsea Flower Show.

In September 2008, the RHS returned to Inner Temple. While the exhibits were of the usual high RHS standard, many of the visitors were struck by the spectacular planting in the High Border. Being some 17 m/56 ft long, it combined annuals such as sweet peas (*Lathyrus odoratus*) with perennials such as asters and rudbeckia. The effect was exuberant and confident, like a horticultural trumpet blast.

In summer, the High Border is dominated by the hot colours of rudbeckia, dahlias, tithonia and cleome, punctuated by fountains of grasses, the dramatic leaves of *Canna* 'Musifolia', tree-like *Dahlia imperialis* and exotic shrubs such as *Amicia zygomeris* and *Tetrapanax papyrifer*. Brunsendorf describes the

High Border as a mosaic of different perennials with pockets of seasonal planting.

The plants take advantage of the mild London microclimate, being surrounded on three sides by buildings, which are single-glazed for conservation reasons. Heat escapes from the centrally heated offices, and the buildings behave like giant radiators, so the main worry for Brunsendorf and her team is not frost, but wind. Strong gusts can barrel in from the Thames and swirl around the garden, so everything in the High Border, where plants such as *Rudbeckia laciniata* 'Herbstsonne' can reach 2.5 m/8 ft, is firmly staked. The effect does not appear at all rigid, however, as one of Brunsendorf's favourite plants, *Persicaria orientalis*, is allowed to arch over the pathway, and the grasses provide movement.

There are two major changeovers in the High Border. At the beginning of late autumn, the herbaceous plants are cut down and the bulb display for the following spring is planted. Then, at the end of late spring, the summer planting, which has meanwhile been growing in the Inner Temple greenhouse and cold frames, is put in. Each changeover takes around six weeks.

Above Beneath the plane trees, head gardener Andrea Brunsendorf has created a Woodland Garden, with ferns and shade-loving perennials such as Japanese anemones and *Persicaria amplexicaulis*.

Top The huge leaves of *Canna* 'Musifolia' look as if they are applauding the colourful display in the High Border.
Above Blocks of colour are used to heighten impact in the High Border.
Left White cosmos, which will flower until the first frosts, here successfully mingles with violet asters.

AVENUE OF PLANE TREES

Opposite the High Border is what used to be a rose garden, with hybrid teas. Brunsendorf has replanted this with English shrub roses, such as *Rosa* Mortimer Sackler, *R.* The Generous Gardener, *R.* Darcey Bussell (their best-flowering rose, apparently) and of course *R.* William Shakespeare. These are underplanted with a carpet of catmint (*Nepeta*).

Either side of the steps that lead down to the main lawn, there is a Mediterranean Garden, where the planting is more relaxed. 'I wanted to have an area where plants are allowed to do what they do naturally,' says Brunsendorf. 'The emphasis is on structure and texture, and we just tidy it up once a year.'

Even so, the selection of plants is impressive. The grasses include *Anemanthele lessoniana*, *Molinia caerulea* subsp. *arundinacea* 'Transparent', and *Stipa ichu* (also known as *Jarava ichu*) – whose white flower heads are a wonderful choice if you want a smaller alternative to cortaderia. Then there is coronilla, caryopteris, verbascum, *Kniphofia rooperi* and, in the centre, a strawberry tree. '*Arbutus unedo*?' I asked. 'No, too boring,' responded Brunsendorf, smiling. 'It's *A. menziesii*.'

The Inner Temple garden is L-shaped, with the main lawn running from the High Border down to the Victoria Embankment, where an avenue of plane trees (*Platanus*) is underplanted with *Liriope muscari* – a tough, dry-shade warrior.

One of the first things that Brunsendorf did when she arrived was to order 13,500 liriopes: 'It took us two months to plant them all, working 2–5 p.m. every day,' she recalled. There is underplanting beneath the trees on the lawn, too – *Hakonechloa macra* and *Polystichum setiferum* 'Herrenhausen', which despite its delicate-looking foliage is remarkably drought-tolerant.

As you turn into the short leg of the L, where there is more shade, the underplanting culminates in a full-scale Woodland Garden, which runs along Kings Bench Walk. There is year-round interest here, from snowdrops (*Galanthus*) in mid-winter, through daffodils (*Narcissus*), tulips (*Tulipa*) and white foxgloves (*Digitalis*), to Japanese anemones (*Anemone* × *hybrida*) and the white spires of *Persicaria amplexicaulis* 'Alba' in late summer and early autumn.

The Peony Garden is here, too, with Chinese tree peonies (*Paeonia suffruticosa*), which have flowers that look as if they are made from magenta tissue paper. In late spring, these are

Above Plants in the High Border are staked to protect them from wind.
Opposite top Dahlias, such as 'Bishop of Llandaff', are favourites.
Opposite right *Calamagrostis* × *acutiflora* 'Karl Foerster' and *Miscanthus nepalensis* compete for attention with *Dahlia* 'Fascination'.
Opposite far right In summer, pots of tender plants such as begonias and solenostemon are grouped at the end of the Kings Bench Walk.

'The High Border is dominated by hot colours, punctuated by fountains of grasses and dramatic leaves.'

accompanied by herbaceous peonies (*P. lactiflora*), *Smyrnium perfoliatum* and *Hesperis matronalis*, while *Hydrangea arborescens* 'Annabelle' takes over in summer, with a backing chorus of bright phloxes and Japanese anemones.

The Woodland Garden leads to in a seasonal pot display at the end of Kings Bench Walk, where Brunsendorf and her team have a chance to try out new combinations – they rearrange the pots four times a year.

Unlike many central London head gardeners, Brunsendorf is fortunate in having quite a bit of backstage space. There are cold frames, a greenhouse and garden offices. One of her main bugbears is maintenance work on the buildings of Inner Temple. 'Scaffolding is a real problem,' she revealed. 'I had to move thirty-six mature hydrangeas in the hottest week of the year, when work started along the west side of the garden.'

Above (clockwise from top left) A spring display of *Papaver somniferum* 'Lauren's Grape' with *Allium* 'Globemaster' and *A.* 'Gladiator'; *Persicaria orientalis* with orange tagetes; *Geranium* Patricia with *Aster amellus* 'Veilchenkönigin'; *Sedum* 'Matrona' with pennisetum.
Right (clockwise from top left) *Persicaria orientalis* with the fast-growing annual climber *Ipomoea lobata*; *Onopordum acanthium* also known as Scotch thistle; *Tithonia rotundifolia* 'Torch'; *Helenium* 'Wesergold'.

CHAPTER TWO
WILD IN THE CITY

CARGO OF COLOUR

DOWNINGS ROADS FLOATING GARDENS, BERMONDSEY

Of all the gardens in this book, the garden barges at Reed's Wharf are the most likely to be swept away. For most of their existence, they have been under threat – not from the river, or a freak tide or an aberrant storm, but from officialdom in one form or another.

The garden barges – or the Downings Roads Floating Gardens at Tower Bridge Moorings, to give them their official name – are the brainchild of architect Nicholas Lacey, and they form what he calls an 'inside-out' London garden square. They are legally moored on what are known as 'ancient moorings', and they comprise seven barges, all planted with trees, shrubs and perennials that provide colour, blossom and berries all year round.

The barges are old Thames lighters – so-called because they 'lightened' the load of seagoing ships bringing cargo into the Port of London. Being built of steel, these barges were the rugged workhorses of the Thames.

Photographs by Marianne Majerus

The purple flowers of *Verbena bonariensis* contrast with a backdrop of golden robinia and Tower Bridge, one of London's best-known landmarks.

OASIS ON THE RIVER

Lacey began his project in the mid-1990s. Even though the trees are visible from the riverside, you really need to step on to this floating oasis to get an idea of the extraordinary scale of the planting.

Each barge has its own character. The first barge, *Medrain*, has a very contemporary mixture of grasses, drought-tolerant perennials such as sedum, and a big bronze phormium. There is *Allium hollandicum* 'Purple Sensation' in spring, and annuals such as cosmos in summer.

The next barge, *Silo*, was the first barge Lacey planted, and it has a formal design of box hedges, softened with roses and honeysuckle (*Lonicera*). At the downstream (eastern) end, there are two crab apples (*Malus*) underplanted with hardy geraniums.

Surpass, at right angles to *Silo*, is one of the two orchard barges. It is planted with an avenue of medlars (*Mespilus germanica*), with more box, flowering perennials such as stachys and helichrysum, and a weeping pear (*Pyrus*).

The other orchard barge, *Surbed*, is at the other end of the square, and has quince (*Cydonia*) trees underplanted with lilac (*Syringa*), choisya and hebe, framed by a golden *Robinia pseudoacacia* 'Frisia'.

Three barges link *Surbed* with *Silo*. At the end is *Sabu*, which is planted with euphorbia, ferns, iris, bergenia and

Verbena bonariensis, framed by more box hedging. By this point the visitor has probably got used to the astonishing number of plants here, but it still comes as a shock to see the white stems of ghost bramble (*Rubus thibetanus*). Many people would think twice about planting this in a big garden, let alone on a barge.

Skua has a weeping birch at either end, and ornamental artichokes (*Cynara cardunculus*), while *Scrip* gives the impression that you have walked off the water and into a country garden. Shrubs such as brachyglottis, choisya and spiraea jostle with Shasta daisies (*Leucanthemum × superbum*) and asters, while hollies (*Ilex*), a *Prunus cerasifera* and another golden robinia provide height. All the barges have ground cover, which is composed of ivy (*Hedera*) and periwinkle (*Vinca*).

Self-sown annuals, such as French marigolds (*Tagetes patula*), nasturtiums (*Tropaeolum majus*) and poppies (*Papaver*), spring up all through the barges, and there are small piles of logs and branches to encourage wildlife. There are even two beehives, complete with buzzing inhabitants, on the medlar orchard barge.

No chemicals are used, and a thick mulch of peat-free compost and manure is put down each year. The gardens are fed with home-made nettle fertilizer, farm manure and organic seaweed products. Now, all this would be impressive enough, but then you realize that the soil is merely one spit deep – in other words, the depth of the metal bit of a spade.

Everything is recycled as far as possible, and collected by the local authority. There is no particular bin day: when it is all ready for collection, someone runs up a flag on the refuse boat.

THE CHANGING WATERWAY

Beneath the planting, the barges are converted into waterborne studio flats. Some of the 100-strong community own their own barges and rent a mooring, while others rent the accommodation on the garden barges. There is very rarely a vacancy, and the inhabitants form what Lacey's wife Teresa calls 'a Noah's Ark of professions'. There is a brain surgeon, two neurologists, an organist and a senior civil servant, as well as a blacksmith, a carpenter and a welder. There are lots of children and lots of cats. So who could possibly object to such a picturesque group? Well, it is a story that is bound up with the changing face of London.

Long gone are the days when the river Thames acted as a sort of motorway for Londoners criss-crossing the capital. The idea of the Archbishop of Canterbury catching a fatal chill as a result of travelling home to Lambeth by barge in freezing cold weather – as happened to Archbishop John Whitgift, who died on 29 February 1604 – would seem unthinkable today.

There is still lots of traffic on the Thames – the tourist boats, and the fast Clipper that takes you from Waterloo to Greenwich, for example. But, in the main, it is merchandise, not the masses,

Opposite The seven barges that house the gardens are Thames lighters, used to reduce the loads of cargo ships arriving at the Port of London.
Top and **above** Annuals such as cosmos and nasturtiums are encouraged to seed themselves in this environment.
Right Teasels vie for attention in front of white asters.

Top There are two orchard barges – one planted with apple trees and one with medlars.
Above Cosmos provides summer-long colour.
Left White asters billow alongside a walkway.
Opposite It is difficult to remember that all the plants, including the trees, are growing in soil only the depth of a spade blade.

that travels by boat. Every day, anything from food, petrol, timber products and cars – from nappies to table tennis bats – is unloaded somewhere along the tidal stretch of the Thames. The London Gateway port, in Thurrock, Essex, which opened in November 2013, is able to accommodate the biggest container ships currently on the seas.

From a pedestrian's point of view, however, it is the riverside, not the waterway, that is busy. You can now walk right along the south side of the river from Butler's Wharf, east of Tower Bridge, to Westminster Bridge, stopping for coffee or lunch at one of the many cafes and restaurants along the way. The route passes some of the most famous London landmarks, such as Tower Bridge, the Tower of London, the grey bulk of HMS *Belfast*, the London Eye, Big Ben and the Houses of Parliament. On both sides of the river, new office and housing developments have sprung up where docks and warehouses once stood derelict, and as a result of this regeneration the area has come under greater official scrutiny.

'*Silo*, the first barge to be planted, has a formal box hedge design, softened with roses and honeysuckle.'

ANCIENT MOORINGS

In 2003, Southwark Borough Council issued eviction notices, giving the barge-dwellers three months to leave, after complaints by residents in the newly built blocks of riverside flats at Chambers Wharf that the boats spoiled their view. The eviction was quashed in 2004, but the Port of London Authority (PLA) then challenged the berth-holders' rights to 'ancient moorings' in court in 2013. The judge threw out the PLA objections, and defined ancient moorings as an 'indeterminate licence', providing that the mooring chains had been in existence before Michaelmas Day (29 September) 1857. Those at Reed's Wharf had been. Sadly, the celebrations were short-lived. Now the barges face a further threat: plans by Thames Water to position one of the drive sites for the new London super-sewer 90 m/295 ft downriver at Chambers Wharf.

In the meantime, life at the floating gardens goes on much as usual. The annual Bonfire Night festivities will be held, as will the Advent lighting-up parties, when the twenty-six residential boats take it in turns to mark each day of Advent by decorating their boats with fairy lights and switching them on.

The impression is of a happy, relaxed community where neighbourhood squabbles are a rarity and residents look out for one another. Perhaps it is the good vibrations that make the plants grow so well in their one spit of soil.

THE OLD CURIOSITY PLOT

MALPLAQUET HOUSE, MILE END

The Mile End Road is not the most obvious place to find a courtyard reminiscent of the glory that was Rome, but Malplaquet House defies any of the usual London stereotypes.

The house is about 90 m/295 ft from Stepney Green underground station, and the wall of the front garden is so high, and so thickly covered with ivy (*Hedera*), jasmine (*Jasminum*) and roses, that it is easy to walk straight past. Until, that is, you catch a glimpse of the house through the front gate.

Two rather sinister eagles – copies of a pair at Knightshayes Court in Devon – stand guard on the brick piers either side of the gate, and the visitor proceeds to the front door under the watchful gaze of a pair of stone dogs, and two sphinxes. On the left, an old war memorial from the village of Marshfield, near Chippenham, looms up from a jungle of fig trees (*Ficus*), olives (*Olea*) and *Trachycarpus fortunei*. Beside it are what look like small tombstones but are actually Yorkshire meerstones, used to mark off mining rights above mineral veins.

Photographs by Marianne Majerus

The obelisk in the front garden at Malplaquet House is a former war memorial from a village in Wiltshire. In front grows *Melianthus major*.

Above the front door, in the window on the first floor, a crucifix is displayed. On the right, beneath the vast leaves of a stooled paulownia, a large stone pedestal, reclaimed from a property in Piccadilly, bears the name 'Tiger'. It is a memorial to a much-loved miniature dachshund that belonged to the current owners, Tim Knox and Todd Longstaffe-Gowan.

Knox is a historian with an art history background. He studied history of art at the Courtauld Institute and has worked as an architectural historian and as head curator for the National Trust. Longstaffe-Gowan studied landscape architecture at Harvard University and completed a PhD in historical geography at University College, London. He describes himself as a gardener and historian, which is a rather modest way of saying that he has advised on the conservation and re-landscaping of some of Britain's most famous gardens. These include Hampton Court (see page 36), Kensington Palace and Southwark Cathedral.

The pair bought Malplaquet House in 1998, from the Spitalfields Trust, and have since worked on its restoration. The main changes were the demolition of the single-storey, flat-roofed shops in front of the house, and the scruffy warehouses behind it. The plants in the front garden grow in what were the cellars of the shops, which have now been filled with earth.

ARTISTIC INTENTIONS

The contrast between the busy Mile End Road and this quiet, green space is dramatic. When the front door opens, and you walk into a hall full of death masks, paintings of saints with eyes upraised to Heaven, and assorted pieces of marble sculpture, you are transported into a world of macabre juxtapositions.

At first glance, the interior of Malplaquet House looks a bit like the Soane Museum in Lincoln's Inn, where Sir John Soane, the architect who designed the Bank of England and Dulwich Picture Gallery, amassed his extraordinary collection of antiquities and works of art. This is not entirely surprising, as Knox was director of the Soane Museum until 2013 (he is now director of the Fitzwilliam Museum in Cambridge), and he and Longstaffe-Gowan have assembled their own huge collection during the past twenty-seven years. However, their artistic intents seem to go beyond a mere arrangement of artefacts. The rooms are works of art in themselves.

In the Sarcophagus Room, for example, there is a massive chimney piece by set designer Christopher Hobbs,

who worked extensively with film directors Ken Russell and Derek Jarman; a collection of portraits of nuns; the lid of the outer coffin of Sasobek, Vizier of Egypt (a copy of the one in the British Museum); and a tabernacle containing the Screaming Skull of Stepney. According to legend, if such skulls are removed from the house or place where they are found, the inhabitants will be haunted by terrible screams.

All of these items would, individually, be fascinating, but together they form something that is more than the sum of its parts, and which is capable of provoking an emotional, almost primitive reaction. One would defy even the most stolid individual not to be slightly taken aback when confronted with a bathroom filled with crucifixes and Victorian memorial pictures that commemorate people who died in horrible accidents.

It is difficult to tear yourself away from these fascinating relics, but the back garden reveals yet more.

STONE CARVINGS

When Malplaquet House was built, between 1741 and 1742, the back garden was 30 m/100 ft long, giving way to fields and meadows. Now much smaller, it is still large enough to have eighteen tree ferns (*Dicksonia antarctica*) creating a feathery canopy beneath the branches of a tall *Robinia pseudoacacia*.

Opposite top The front door is guarded by two stone dogs.
Opposite far left Reclaimed stone gives the impression of tombstones.
Opposite left A sphinx lurks half-buried by plants.
Above The Chusan palm adds an exotic flavour to the front garden.

(The tallest of the tree ferns was planted roughly when the house was built.) The owners' intention was to create a fernery, and you feel that, if someone were to build a roof across the 4-m/13-ft brick walls that surround the planting on three sides, it would be like standing in a giant Wardian case.

There are smaller ferns, such as *Dryopteris sieboldii* and *Asplenium scolopendrium*, growing among *Acanthus mollis* and hydrangea, while an enormous *Actinidia arguta* snakes in and out of the tree ferns. Here also are more stone carvings and statues – a figure of the dead Christ lies on the ground beneath a della Robbia-style plaque of a bishop, while another figure of an old man – a prophet, or a philosopher, perhaps – stands surrounded by antlers and giant clam shells. The standing figure comes from a frieze designed by James Bubb in the early nineteenth century, illustrating the origins and progress of music, which once decorated the Regency facade of the Italian Opera House in Haymarket, on the site of what is now Her Majesty's Theatre.

The rest of the original garden is now the site of a sheltered housing development, yet within the high walls of Malplaquet's courtyard it is difficult to remember you are next door to a block of flats. It is more like being in Rome, in an ancient shady courtyard designed as a refuge from the hot summer sun. Scraps of Italian conversation, from the Eritrean family next door, help foster this illusion.

It is interesting to see how the antlers and the shells undergo a kind of metamorphosis in this crepuscular atmosphere. The antlers look more like branches or ferns, particularly the flatter antlers, which give the impression of being fossilized versions of their namesake, the staghorn fern (*Platycerium*). The shells, so often used in seaside cottage decor, look more like strange carvings.

Knox and Longstaffe-Gowan have plans to create some kind of dripping grotto opposite the back door, which can only help to heighten the effect of crumbling grandeur.

'A figure of the dead Christ lies on the ground beneath the fronds of *Dicksonia antarctica*.'

Above Eighteen tree ferns – one as old as the house itself – provide a feathery canopy for the back garden.
Right (clockwise from top left) A figure of the dead Christ; the skull of a deer hangs on a wall; antlers in an old washtub take on the appearance of strange growths; tree ferns thriving in the shelter of the high walls.

EXOTIC HIDEAWAY

PETHERTON ROAD, ISLINGTON

Someone once told garden designer Declan Buckley that, if you wanted an indication as to the sort of job you would enjoy as an adult, you should look at the things that fascinated you as a child. In Buckley's case, that was the greenhouse at his family home in County Cork, in the Republic of Ireland, where he grew cacti and other exotica, and pestered the staff in the local garden centres and nurseries for advice and information. Today, his metropolitan version of that greenhouse is a glazed conservatory at the rear of his Islington flat. It looks out on to a green canopy that is more like North Vietnam than north London.

It is a common misconception that London gardeners are somehow restricted by their urban surroundings and lack of space. True, there is not much you can do about a high wall, or a tall building next door, or that sycamore (*Acer pseudoplatanus*) seedling that the neighbours failed to notice before it was big enough to blot out half the sky, and wide enough of girth to merit a Tree Preservation Order.

There are compensations, however. It is very rare to feel that you have a garden that just relates to the surrounding landscape,

as you would, say, in the Yorkshire Dales or the Cotswolds. The result is a delightful miscellany of fantasy made real: Moroccan courtyards, Tuscan-style olives and cypresses, Versailles-inspired parterres, and sleek outdoor spaces in which James Bond himself would be proud to barbecue a burger.

London gardeners are inventive, and will press into service trellis, mirrors, balconies and window boxes in an effort to transform their plots from mundane to magical. Nature is on their side, too. You can be a bit more adventurous in your choices when it comes to growing subtropical plants, because London is an urban heat island, and temperatures can be up to 8°C/15°F higher than in the surrounding countryside.

MARITIME CLIMATE

American gardeners often ask which US hardiness zones equate to the UK. London is allegedly the equivalent of Zone 9 in the US, which puts it on a par with San Antonio, New Orleans and San Francisco. However, just as any American gardener will be able to tell you instantly whether they are in Zone 7 (Richmond, Virginia) or Zone 10 (San Diego, California), they will also tell you that the hardiness zone is only part of the story. It is an important part – it basically tells you which plants are going to get through the winter – but it does not take into account humidity, snow cover, light levels and so on.

Photographs by Marianne Majerus

There is a wonderful view looking down on the garden, with canopies of *Eriobotrya japonica, Fatsia polycarpa, Schefflera alpina*, the new shoots of *Tetrapanax papyrifer* and *Pseudopanax chathamicus.*

Being a group of islands, the UK benefits from a temperate maritime climate, and this becomes more pronounced the closer to the coast you are. On the other hand, the light levels can never compare, even in the south of the UK, with those in California or the southern Mediterranean. Thus, a plant such as *Campsis grandiflora*, which will grow quite happily in a sheltered London garden, may not get around to showing off its orange trumpet flowers before the first frosts of autumn, unless the summer has been particularly hot and sunny.

However, the idea of coming home to a Thai jungle or an oasis of huge green leaves after a long day at the office (and what seemed like an even longer journey on public transport) is therapeutic to say the least, and this partly explains the increasing popularity of subtropical plants and gardening styles in the UK.

PLANTS FOR PRIVACY

Buckley is reluctant to be labelled as an exotics specialist – his portfolio encompasses styles from traditional English to minimalist contemporary. Yet you have only to look at his garden's jungle-effect design as well as the specimens growing there to realize that Buckley is a plantaholic.

Take his scheffleras, for example. There are at least three species: *S. alpina* (with seed heads that look like mini sputniks), *S. taiwaniana* (with its delicate slender leaves) and *S. fantsipanensis* (from northern Vietnam, whose leaves grow in a two-tiered effect). Among them, competing for canopy space, are *Tetrapanax papyrifer* 'Rex', loquats (*Eriobotrya japonica*) and pseudopanax.

Buckley particularly recommends his pseudopanax for city gardens, and there are certainly enough species to suit every taste. He has *P. arboreus* (now generally known as *Neopanax arboreus*, which has glossy green leaves and attractive seed heads), *P. crassifolius* (which grows naturally into a tall lollipop shape as a defence against the now-extinct herbivorous moa) and toothed lancewood (*P. ferox*), with its weird, downward-pointing leaves.

Even the fatsia is not the usual *F. japonica*, but *F. polycarpa*, which has finer-cut leaves. Similarly, the trachycarpus is *T. wagnerianus*, whose fans naturally grow in a more layered, formal manner than *T. fortunei*.

Here also is to be found *Daphniphyllum macropodum*, with its red stems and flower heads, which has a reputation for being tender. In fact, it is hardy in the UK (Angus White, owner of the

Above A formal paved path leads the eye through the garden.
Right above The orange cushions on the metal garden chairs introduce a flash of colour in a sea of green.
Right and **far right** The huge leaves of tetrapanax and tree ferns provide privacy as well as creating an exotic jungle ambience.

exotics nursery Architectural Plants, describes it as 'tough as old boots'), but it prefers a sheltered woodland site. It is a good tree for a small space such as here at Petherton Road, because it has a neat growth habit.

Below all these exotics, the understorey contains equally fascinating treasures. There is *Disporum longistylum*, discovered by the American plant hunter Dan Hinkley in Sichuan, China. With its bamboo-like stems, green leaves and white flowers, it looks like a large shrubby version of Solomon's seal (*Polygonatum*).

Disporopsis pernyi, another Chinese native, also looks a little bit like Solomon's seal – its common name is evergreen Solomon's seal – but its stems are more erect, and the white flowers are lemon-scented and more bell-like. It is hardy, and a good woodland garden performer.

Iris confusa is regarded with suspicion by many gardeners as it has the reputation for being a bit of a thug. It is, however, a most elegant thug, with white flowers, and arching leaves that are very different from the rigid foliage of other iris species. In any case, you need a certain amount of thuggishness in subtropical gardens, because only vigorous plants will survive in the deep shade formed by the canopy of huge leaves above.

This canopy, while beautiful in its own right, also serves a practical purpose. Buckley's garden, like so many in London, is overlooked by neighbours in every direction. At night, when the garden lights are on, and the big leaves screen out the surrounding houses and muffle the usual noises of the city, it is a private paradise. The canopy has its uses, too, in daylight hours. Buckley has an ingenious device that switches the water supply from the shower in the bathroom (just inside the back door) to an outside shower, below the steps that lead up to the first-floor conservatory. He can take a shower in complete privacy, surrounded by the scented flowers of *Holboellia latifolia* and *Trachelospermum jasminoides*, while the early morning sun makes rainbows in the spray.

Left (clockwise from top) *Fatsia polycarpa* has longer, more elegant leaves than *F. japonica*, but is just as hardy; an African walking stick is one of the many interesting objects in the garden; Buckley's outdoor shower.
Above left The giant leaves of an ornamental rhubarb.
Above right and **below right** Eye-catching are *Fatsia polycarpa* silhouetted against the sky as well as the strange leaves of the toothed lancewood.

'Below the canopy of leaves, the understorey contains equally fascinating treasures.'

COUNTRY LIFE

THE OLD VICARAGE, PETERSHAM

Vicarages, in the British imagination, tend to come in two varieties. There is the iconic Queen Anne or Georgian species, dating from the time when the local lord of the manor had the power of appointing the parish priest (usually the younger son of a well-to-do family). Typically, a vicarage from this period looks like an elegant doll's house, with the front door in the middle, multi-paned windows on either side, and garlands of wisteria hanging from its mellow walls.

Then there is the Victorian vicarage, which is usually built of red brick or grey stone, with high ceilings and a multiplicity of gables and bay windows. No one – unless they were catering for the needs of a Victorian rector with ten children – would build such a house today. However, just such a house was constructed c.1899 as the vicarage of All Saints Church in the little village of Petersham.

The church, which was dedicated but never consecrated, was designed by the architect John Kelly, who specialized in a style described by Nikolaus Pevsner as 'emphatically Italian Early Christian or Romanesque'. It has an extraordinary

Photographs by Hugo Rittson Thomas

Hollyhocks in luscious summer berry colours stand either side of the path, while cranesbill and lady's mantle billow across the herringbone brick.

36-m/118-ft campanile, or bell tower, surmounted by the statue of a saint. The church itself is now a private residence.

WILDERNESS APPROACH

You can see the church and its campanile from the gardens of The Old Vicarage, and their monumental scale might have had a rather sobering effect on the current inhabitants, were it not for the fact that the garden has been cleverly designed to give an impression of rural intimacy rather than ecclesiastical pomp and circumstance. The owners of The Old Vicarage had wanted a country garden – something that was verging on wilderness and in which there had been as little intervention in the way of chemicals as possible. Altogether the garden extends to 1.25 hectares/3 acres – very large for a London garden, even in a suburb such as Petersham.

The garden around the house is a Cutting Garden, a feature that is normally tucked away out of sight along with the garden shed and greenhouse. Here, Mary Keen and Pip Morrison of Designed Landscapes created rectangular beds within a framework of herringbone brick paths, which imposes a formality on the billowing beds of flowers and vegetables.

A picket fence painted in a subtle off-white encloses this part of the garden, while a long herringbone brick path leads

down to the main gate through a meadow, lined on either side by an avenue of heirloom apple trees. The long path helps relate the rest of the garden to the area around the house, and to retain a sense of scale – not an easy task, given the preposterous campanile next door.

At the rear of the house, a generous terrace reverses the design, with herringbone rectangles set in a grid of stone paving, echoing the beds at the front. Grecian pots and an old washing copper provide informal containers, while roses and clematis climb the walls of the house.

VEGETABLE PATCH

There are two changeovers in the cutting beds each year, explained head gardener Matt Collins. Spring bulbs such as daffodils and tulips make way for summer bedding such as dahlias, *Tithonia rotundifolia* and cosmos amid cranesbill (*Geranium*) and salvias. In winter, the beds are left bare until the first bulbs come up; meanwhile, the design of the hard landscaping provides pattern and interest of its own.

Right at the front, in pride of place by the garden gate, is the vegetable patch, with runner beans, chard and courgettes edged with nasturtiums (*Tropaeolum*) and calendula.

The overall effect is unapologetically pretty and incredibly colourful. It looks a little bit like Monet's paintings of his garden at Giverny – relaxed, sunny, informal, productive. The notions of 'good taste' and colour coordination become irrelevant; the impact depends on a happy jumble of flowers.

WINTER SCENT

Behind the house, two all-weather rattan loungers sit in the shade of a large black locust (*Robinia pseudoacacia*). They have a grandstand view of the football goal on the other side of the lawn, while behind them a grass path leads through a Winter Garden, where the scent of winter-flowering shrubs such as mahonia and sarcococca can linger in the green corridor formed by neighbouring trees and shrubs. There are foxgloves (*Digitalis*) here too, as well as periwinkle (*Vinca*), *Geranium phaeum* and hellebores, while spotted laurels (*Aucuba japonica*) give the impression of dappled sunlight.

'The overall effect is unapologetically pretty and incredibly colourful - a happy jumble of flowers.'

Opposite In spring, tulips provide a colourful display, and the grid system of the Cutting Garden beds is clearly visible.

Top By midsummer, the beds have all but disappeared beneath a profusion of flowers, but the paths still allow easy access.

Above (clockwise from top left) White hollyhocks, forget-me-nots and dahlias all flourish at The Old Vicarage.

Right The path extends through a meadow planted with apple trees.

Right A tree house provides the ideal environment for children.
Below Planting beneath the trees helps make the transition from formal lawn to woodland wilderness.
Bottom Much of the large garden is woodland, providing a habitat for wildlife including songbirds, squirrels and badgers.

The path leads to the greenhouse, where Collins sows most of the plants for the Cutting Garden, before giving way to woodland. You cannot see the wall that divides the garden from Richmond Park behind it, but you can see glimpses of the park itself. The grass on that side, grazed short by herds of deer in the former royal hunting ground, is the only clue that the two areas are separate.

A spectacular tree house – more of a village than a single dwelling – dominates the back of the garden, which in late spring is a blur of pink, white, yellow and blue. Pink campion (*Silene*), cow parsley (*Anthriscus sylvestris*), greater celandine (*Chelidonium majus*) and alkanet (*Alkanna tinctoria*) grow with wild abandon, and Collins simply outlines paths with logs and keeps them strimmed to make walking easier. It is a good technique to copy if you have a large area of wild garden.

Originally, there were elms (*Ulmus*), but these were lost when Dutch elm disease took hold in the 1970s. In their place is black locust, a North American native which thrives in London, shrugs off pollution and also makes a good substitute for ash,

under threat from the *Chalara fraxinea* fungus. Black locust suckers like mad, so it is not a choice for a small garden, but its wood provides good firewood and its scented flowers attract foraging bees.

WILDLIFE HABITAT

As for other wildlife, there is always something moving in The Old Vicarage garden: the twitch of a squirrel's tail as it runs up a tree, the flicker and rustle of a robin or blackbird investigating the leaf litter, or the restless quiver of a dragonfly poised above the pond.

Collins has seen evidence of badgers, and there are grass snakes, stag beetles and woodpeckers, both green and greater spotted. Thanks to the high wall, the deer in Richmond Park are unable to get into the garden and eat everything in sight, but nuthatches, a bird that is not often seen in London because they prefer mature woodland, bear witness to the success of the surrounding habitat.

The owners' Buff Orpington chickens, which live in a run near the shed and compost heaps, also seem to enjoy the chance to return to their jungle fowl roots, scratching contentedly among the shrubs and trees. They seem to epitomize the rural ambience that Mary Keen, Pip Morrison and the owners of The Old Vicarage have managed so successfully to foster here.

Above The pond is designed to attract wildlife, with lots of marginal plants that offer shelter for frogs and dragonflies. The hut beyond the pond houses the family's collection of tortoises, and this informal area is also home to Buff Orpington chickens.

OLYMPIC LEGACY

QUEEN ELIZABETH OLYMPIC PARK, STRATFORD

Surprisingly for a nation that has been trying to boss the rest of the world around for several centuries, the British do not tend to have much faith in the ability of their own governments or institutions to organize anything. The London 2012 Olympics, therefore, came as something of a pleasant shock. It took place on schedule, Team GB won lots of gold medals, and everyone seemed to enjoy it. Even better, much of the enjoyment was provided by the planting in the Olympic Park. Colleagues and friends who previously had never expressed any interest in horticulture whatsoever came home from an Olympic event raving about the meadows filled with colourful flowers.

INFORMAL LANDSCAPE

The Olympic Park (or the Queen Elizabeth Olympic Park, as it is now officially known) covers the original Olympic site and contains many of the same features, such as the landscaping. At 227 hectares/560 acres, it is the same size as Hyde Park (although it feels larger) and it has been one of the biggest urban park projects in Europe for 150 years.

Photographs by Marianne Majerus

In one of the iconic pictorial meadows can be found *Hordeum jubatum, Centaurea cyanus, Agrostemma githago* amd *Eschscholzia californica.*

The site divides roughly into two halves – north and south. The southern section, around the Olympic Stadium, contains the 2012 Gardens, inspired by the native plants of Europe, North America, the southern hemisphere and Asia.

Alongside the stadium are the new Pleasure Gardens, designed by (among others) Piet Oudolf and James Corner Field Operations, who did the High Line in New York. The Pleasure Gardens are, as the name suggests, areas for play of all kinds, with carousels, climbing walls, playground and performance spaces.

Indeed, the park does children's playgrounds really well. In the shadow of the ArcelorMittal Orbit, designed by Sir Anish Kapoor, is one of the most popular areas for families – the fountains. Here, 195 computer-controlled water jets shoot up from the pavement at different heights and different times. A long curving bench provides plenty of space for parents and grandparents to sit, and somewhere to park buggies and other paraphernalia, and the bench follows the sinuous line of an avenue of *Prunus serrula*, which helps give a sense of shelter. The jets of water come and go while small people run through them shrieking with excitement. Even if you do not have children with you, it is fun to watch.

Tumbling Bay, the children's playground by the Timber Lodge, is even more fun, with a system of water pumps and

dams that are hand-operated and allow you to send miniature tributaries running down a selection of channels to a paddling pool. There are wobbly bridges, tree houses and sandpits, set within a natural, informal landscape of trees and grasses.

The river Lea and its various branches form a tracery of waterways through the park, and the northern section contains a wetlands area designed to showcase and encourage the various forms of wildlife that inhabit London's rivers and canals.

Hopkins' Field and Alfred's Meadow, in front of the Copper Box arena, are designed to be meadows, lawns or venues, as needed. Hopkins' Field has an oak tree at its heart, and is sown with meadow plants, such as daisy (*Bellis*), hawkbit (*Leontodon*) and red clover (*Trifolium pratense*). It was named in memory of the landscape architect John Hopkins, who designed and oversaw the creation of the green spaces enjoyed by visitors to the London 2012 Olympic and Paralympic Games.

RURAL RETREAT

The park will be a work in progress for some years to come. The Olympic Stadium closed in 2013 for three-year renovation work, and at times other construction projects, including housing developments, can give the area the atmosphere of a building site.

There are vast expanses of hard landscaping (to allow for the movement of huge crowds), which reflect back the heat on a hot day. On a cold day, only the sporting arenas, and the comforting monoliths of John Lewis and Marks and Spencer over at the Westfield shopping centre, stand in the way of any sharp, east wind blowing in from the Thames estuary.

The balance between the wide walkways and roads, and the planting, is always going to be skewed, because the stadiums are still used as venues. However, some areas have been reclaimed for planting since the Olympics themselves.

The Pleasure Gardens have been built on what was formerly the main pedestrian plaza, and alongside them there are trees, and lots of refreshment stands, serving drinks and snacks. Benches and even wooden loungers – very like those on the High Line in New York – provide an opportunity to sit down.

The Great British Gardens, behind the Olympic Stadium, represent gold, silver and bronze, and were designed by twelve-year-old Hannah Clegg, from Wiltshire, and Rachel Read, an occupational therapist from Essex. It is like a little rural retreat, with a wildlife pond, fruit trees and woven archways leading from one section to the other. It is a very pleasant space, and the human sundial in the silver section is fun (on a sunny day). However, unless you are aware of the concept behind the overall design, it does not really make obvious sense.

Opposite Take a moment to enjoy the view across the wet woodland area.
Top Echinacea and veronicastrum thrive in the North America Garden.
Above Seek out *Lilium* 'Sweet Surrender' in the Asia Garden.
Right *Ligusticum lucidum* is native to Spain.
Following pages This glorious planting is part of the Europe Garden and
includes *Stipa calamagrostis* and *Leucanthemum* × *superbum* 'T.E. Killin'.

Top The colourful hoardings are no match for the vivid shades of the flowers, including *Allium* 'Globemaster' and *Viscaria oculata*.
Above and **left** Swathes of *Eschscholzia californica* soften the straight lines of the stone gabion walls.
Opposite The wetlands area is designed to showcase and encourage the wildlife that inhabits London's rivers and canals.

It would be nice to have an information board explaining the ideas behind the garden. Admittedly, there are lots of signs in this part of the park, but they all say: 'Please do not pick the fruit because it damages the trees.'

URBAN ENVIRONMENTS
Neither is there much information about the 2012 Gardens. Small signs in the various beds state facts such as 'southern hemisphere' or 'North America', but there is no information board to explain that they represent a timeline of plant introductions (from Europe through to Asia).

Three of the UK's most influential landscape designers worked on these beds. Professor Nigel Dunnett and Professor James Hitchmough of Sheffield University have arguably done more than anyone else in the UK to make people aware of new ways of planting urban environments. Green roofs, pictorial meadows and rain gardens are all now familiar terms among the wider public – not just gardeners – thanks to their work. Garden designer Sarah Price, who won a gold medal at the 2012 Chelsea Flower Show for her *Daily Telegraph* garden, and is a visiting lecturer in garden design at Sheffield, was also part of the design team, bringing her distinctive elegant style to the planting.

An information board giving credit to these individuals, and explaining the concept behind the beds, would not only be useful but would also provide an opportunity to tell overseas visitors about British horticultural talent, which is admired the world over.

There are no lists of plant names, not even on a sheet at the information centre, or on the website. This could be because the plants are always changing (there are two changeovers a year), but it is fairly easy to update a web page or a loose-leaf laminated directory. The High Line in New York supplies planting information particularly well.

This lack of visitor information at the Queen Elizabeth Olympic Park is a huge shame, because the planting is fabulous. It is so marvellous that you forget your tired feet, and follow the sinuous curves of the landscaping to see yet more grasses, yet more perennials, yet more contrast in form and texture. It is like having a masterclass in the New Perennial style – and in a way that is exactly what it is.

'Three of the UK's most influential landscape designers planned the schemes for the borders.'

PERFECTION IN MINIATURE

REGINA ROAD, FINSBURY PARK

Mark Winstanley thought his back garden in Finsbury Park was too small to be of interest to a garden designer. It is a typical London plot, 5 m × 22 m/17 ft × 72 ft long, set behind an elegant Victorian terraced house in a leafy street. The house itself had been extended at the back to provide a glassed-in dining area beside the kitchen, with a huge glazed door about 2.5-m/8-ft square opening out on to the garden.

In summer, a wooden trellis or screen forms a pergola above this area, but in winter, when the door is shut, two hydraulic hinges allow the trellis to be flipped down – a bit like a garage door – to form a screen. It is an extremely clever arrangement, and as a result of this design the back of the house forms a series of cubes.

In 2012, Winstanley decided to turn his attention to the back garden:

I jokingly asked my then partner who would be their dream designer to do the garden. We started throwing in a few names, and Bunny Guinness was the name we kept

Photographs by Marianne Majerus

A tall yew hedge has created two distinct areas in this north London garden. Openings in the hedge allow glimpses of the other part.

coming back to. We did not know her – although we had heard her on the radio, doing *Gardeners' Question Time* – so we had a look at her website, and sent her an email asking her if she would like to come and see us. We thought she would say 'No', but to our surprise she said 'Yes'.

Guinness began by coming to spend the day in the garden. 'She was doing her own sort of brainstorming, just reacting to it,' recalls Winstanley. 'We made her lots of cups of tea, and she showed us her ideas and we discussed them, and she then went back to the office and drew them up.' Some designers need to lie down in a darkened room at the mere thought of doing a London garden, but Guinness says she loves them:

London has a lovely climate, and the gardens and clients are all so different. I have lots of 'repeat offenders', because everyone in London moves so much. If I have worked with a client once, the second time round is more relaxed because you have more confidence in each other. I like to work with the client, to sketch out ideas on the kitchen table. It is the same if I'm doing a 100-acre job – it speeds the process up. By the time we have finished, the plan is more or less complete – all I have to do is a scale plan and put in the construction details.

Left Straight lines and symmetry create a sense of order that makes the garden feel more spacious.
Top Standard medlars crop prolifically each year.
Above Matching benches face each other across the Indian firebowl.

Guinness may like London projects, but she admits that they can have their tricky moments:

> I have been doing this job for forty years, and every time you come across some problem you have never encountered. Often you have got covenants [legal restrictions], and you have to think about irrigation, loading – especially for roof terraces and basements – and planning. And blocking off roads [in order to crane materials into a garden] is a nightmare.

Winstanley did not have any particular brief for the garden, but he was keen to incorporate a wooden figure, commissioned by his aunt in Derbyshire, and carved from an oak gatepost. It has the look of an antique 'term' (from the Latin 'terminus', meaning 'end' or 'boundary'), the name given to a sculpted figure, usually just head and shoulders, set on a pillar or column. Guinness sited the Pan-like figure against a yew (*Taxus*) hedge that Winstanley had already planted across the garden, about two-thirds of the way down it, with an opening on either side.

If you walk through one of the archways in the yew hedge, there is a pond brimming with water lilies (*Nymphaea*) and pickerel weed (*Pontederia*). This area gets the morning sun, and it is a good place to have breakfast and read the paper.

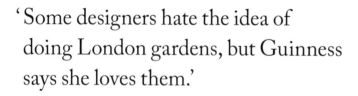

'Some designers hate the idea of doing London gardens, but Guinness says she loves them.'

RIPE MEDLARS

The first part of the garden is quite formal, with lots of straight lines. Guinness continued the cubic theme into the hard landscaping, with paving made of limestone setts, while square French oak beams created four raised beds for clipped box (*Buxus*) and standard medlars (*Mespilus germanica*).

On either side, as you step into the garden, there are two pomegranate trees (*Punica granatum*) in terracotta pots, while further down two all-weather rattan sofas face each other across an antique kadhai (Indian firebowl). The pomegranates grow well in London, since they like sunny, sheltered sites that are not waterlogged, but they have not fruited yet. The pots are specially designed to allow the roots to go through the bottom and down into the soil beneath.

The medlars, on the other hand, fruit prolifically. The fruit looks a bit like a cross between an apple and a big, brown rosehip. When picked – ideally after the first frost – the fruit is not supposed to be eaten until it has rotted, or 'bletted'. No wonder D.H. Lawrence

referred to them as 'wineskins of brown morbidity' in his poem 'Medlars and Sorb-Apples'.

The term 'bletted' is said to have been invented by the English botanist John Lindley, and opinion is divided over whether you should leave the medlars on the tree to blet, or whether you should pick them first and store them. Traditionally, they are stored in sawdust or bran. Whatever you do, wait until they are brown and squishy before eating.

Winstanley enjoys eating ripe medlars (which are said to be an acquired taste, with vaguely cinnamon-like overtones), but he also makes medlar jelly, which is cooked in the same way as crab-apple jelly, and has a similar, rosy-red colour. It seems strange to be talking about medlars in a London garden, but that is the magic of good garden design; it transports you to a different place. This effect at Regina Road is enhanced by the figure of Pan against its dark screen of yew, and the kadhai burning in the foreground, recreating the atmosphere of a pagan temple or some other ancient place of ritual.

Above left The pebble path in the further part of the garden provides a textural contrast to the square sett paving nearer the house.
Above right The figure of Pan comes from Derbyshire. It is carved from an old gatepost and was commissioned by the owner's aunt.

CHAPTER THREE
GARDENERS' WORLDS

FLOWERS AS THERAPY

OLD ENGLISH GARDEN, BATTERSEA PARK

Many Londoners tend to think of Battersea Park as dating from the Festival of Britain in 1951, because the Festival Pleasure Gardens were built at Battersea as part of the celebrations. This festival had been planned as early as 1943 to mark the centenary of the Great Exhibition held in London in 1851. When the Second World War ended in 1945, the British government under Prime Minister Clement Attlee saw the festival as a good opportunity to promote the British contribution to science, technology and the arts.

Some of the best-known names from the creative arts were recruited: at Battersea, the creation of the Pleasure Gardens was supervised by the artist John Piper and his great friend, the cartoonist Osbert Lancaster, who designed the Fountain Lake and the Grand Vista. The Flower Gardens were designed by Russell Page. A huge funfair dominated rail commuters' view of the park as they gazed out of the window on the approach to Victoria station – the Big Dipper ran along one entire side of the park until the funfair closed in 1974.

Photographs by Marianne Majerus

Centranthus ruber 'Albus' and *Lilium regale* with salvia and cranesbill grow in the Old English Garden, which was designed by Sarah Price.

In fact, like any self-respecting London institution, Battersea Park's history goes further back than one might imagine. Since it was first created, it has always been very much a people's park. It was officially opened by Queen Victoria in 1858, on a site reclaimed from Thames marshland, which had been shored up with material excavated from the building of Surrey Docks. This was supplied by Thomas Cubitt, a master builder, who financed his contribution to the park, and the reclamation of the Thames embankment, from the mansion flats he built in Prince of Wales Drive and Albert Bridge Road.

Cubitt was an extraordinary character. He had a great interest in the arts, particularly literature, and his clients included Charles Dickens and Thomas Carlyle. He built the east front of Buckingham Palace, which includes the famous balcony. A great friend of the royal family, particularly Prince Albert, Cubitt shared his royal patron's interest in improving the city environment for its continuously expanding workforce. It is easy, therefore, to imagine him approving wholeheartedly the current Thrive project in Battersea Park.

Thrive arrived at Battersea Park in 2002, and now have three gardens there, including the Old English Garden. Funding for the gardens, and for their maintenance, has been met by Jo Malone Limited, the luxury fragrance brand founded by British parfumier Jo Malone and now owned by Estée Lauder.

HORTICULTURAL THERAPY

Thrive is a charity that provides horticultural training and therapy to gardeners with physical disabilities or mental health issues. It was the brainchild of a horticulturist called Chris Underhill, who had been inspired by his work with people with learning disabilities. Underhill's work was funded by, among others, Dr Geoffrey Udall, a paediatrician, who in 1989 bequeathed his family's estate and 1.25-hectare/3-acre Walled Garden at Beech Hill, near Reading, as a national headquarters and training garden.

Their collaboration became the charity Thrive in 1998 and it is now responsible not only for the Reading garden and the Old English Garden in Battersea Park but also for two more gardens – at King's Heath in Birmingham, and Saltwell, in Gateshead. Udall's bequests still help to fund its work, and it provides training and advice for people with all kinds of disabilities, ranging from stroke or heart disease, dementia and visual impairment. The Battersea project alone provides horticultural therapy to more than 200 disabled people.

Thrive have been looking after the Old English Garden since 2009. In 2012, it was redesigned by Sarah Price, an award-winning garden designer who was part of the team responsible for the 2012 beds at the Queen Elizabeth Olympic Park (see page 82).

ROMANTIC TEXTURE

The Old English Garden has always been a popular spot within Battersea Park. It has a formal pond surrounded by beds of shrubs and perennials and a pergola, and benches sheltered by thick hedges. This sun trap on the north side of the park, near the Albert Bridge gate, was, however, tucked away behind shrubs and fencing, so unless you knew it was there it was not that easy to find.

Old postcards of the garden show it variously as: an old-fashioned rose garden (that is, with no planting other than roses) with women in Edwardian hats and men in boaters sitting on the benches; a more herbaceous garden, with pots of hostas and hollyhocks (*Alcea*) in the borders; and a 1960s garden full of bright summer bedding. Immediately before Price's redesign, it had been a slightly overgrown, traditional English garden, with a wisteria-clad pergola and various bits of herbaceous planting but without any real sense of cohesion or concept.

Today, the Old English Garden is a romantic, scented garden full of old-fashioned shrub roses, honeysuckle (*Lonicera*) and jasmine, but with swathes of perennials pulling the garden together and providing a soft, romantic texture.

The women in the Edwardian hats and the chaps in the boaters would still recognize the basic layout: the pergola is there, as is the pond and the fountain. But the slight rigidity

Opposite Roses help conjure a romantic atmosphere.
Top *Digitalis lutea* rises up in front of a wisteria-draped pergola.
Above *Salvia nemorosa* 'Caradonna' grows happily among *Geranium* 'Ann Folkard'.
Left Here, *Salvia nemorosa* 'Caradonna' has been planted alongside *Verbena bonariensis*.

that always seems to afflict formal park gardens has gone, and in its place are the sort of plants that have now become part of the traditional English garden vocabulary.

Hardy geraniums include *G.* 'Ann Folkard', *G. psilostemon* and *G. × oxonianum*. There are the blue-purple spires of *Salvia nemorosa* 'Caradonna', as well as *Digitalis lutea*, with its delicate, yellow flowers. *Papaver somniferum* grows alongside *Eupatorium maculatum*, while *Valeriana officinalis* and *Centranthus ruber* 'Albus' billow out above reclaimed brick paths.

Baltic parsley (*Cenolophium denudatum*), a useful umbellifer for the late summer garden, is also used extensively here, as is *Veronicastrum virginicum* 'Album' and the white, foaming flowers of *Persicaria polymorpha*, which reach 1.75 m/6 ft.

THE OTHER TWO THRIVE GARDENS

Originally, the Thrive base at Battersea Park was the Herb Garden, which has been transformed from a derelict space and now includes culinary, medicinal and therapeutic plants. The focal point is an Alitex greenhouse, which is used for propagation and for tender plants such as salads and tomatoes.

The third, and newest, garden is the Main Garden, which includes a new building designed by architects Pedder & Scampton. This replaces the portable buildings that – as so often happens – were outgrown long ago, and takes the form of a

curved structure, built around a large plane tree. Work started in October 2013, and Price meanwhile designed the landscaping.

The roof and rear wall of the building are covered in slate, while at the front, on the inside of the curve, there is a glass-walled orangery. This has been designed as a workroom, and big open doors allow the gardeners to come and go all day without needing to worry about shutting doors or wiping boots. Tool stores have been built into the external walls.

NATURAL ATTRACTION

Horticulture as therapy has a long history. In 1798, Dr Benjamin Rush, one of the signatories of the American Declaration of Independence, recorded that gardening improved the conditions of mentally ill patients. Gardening as a means of physical and occupational rehabilitation was also used by the US Veterans Administration to help soldiers returning from combat after the Second World War.

'It is a romantic, scented garden, with swathes of perennials providing a soft texture.'

In 1984, the American biologist Edward O. Wilson published his book *Biophilia*, inspired by a theory first put forward by the German psychoanalyst Erich Fromm that human beings are naturally attracted to other forms of life. This love has an important biological and evolutionary purpose, argued Wilson, in that it drives us to nurture animals and plants, which provide food and other benefits.

Any gardener will tell you that a couple of hours pottering around is therapeutic. Tasks such as sowing seeds, propagating and deadheading do not require complicated decision-making, so they are non-stressful. In addition, like Sarah Price's Old English Garden, they offer a tangible, pleasing result.

Opposite Reclaimed brick paving leads to an armillary sphere. The white fluffy flower heads are those of *Persicaria polymorpha*.
Above Purple spheres of *Allium cristophii* nestle among *Geranium* 'Ann Folkard' and *Centranthus ruber* 'Albus'.
Right The fountain at the centre of the formal pond, seen here framed by the pergola, is part of the original design for the garden.

THE HEALING GARDEN

ROYAL COLLEGE OF PHYSICIANS, MARYLEBONE

It would be too fanciful to say that you can sense the ghosts of long-dead physicians looking over your shoulder as you wander round the gardens of the Royal College of Physicians (RCP). You may find, however, that you suddenly become acutely aware of the knowledge, acquired over the millennia by experiment and often by chance, that lies behind the wealth of plants in this living museum.

Represented here in plant form are the great healers of history. Dioscorides, the Greek physician who wrote *De Materia Medica*, a five-volume pharmacopoeia used for 1,500 years until supplanted by more modern herbals in the fifteenth and sixteenth centuries; William Harvey, who discovered the way the body's circulation works; Nicholas Culpeper, whose *Herbal* brought the use of plants as medicines to an English-speaking audience; and Olof Rudbeck, who discovered the human lymphatic system and whose son taught Carl Linnaeus.

All these figures leap into focus as you examine the plants they used, the plants that they misunderstood, the plants that were named after them and the plants that still form the basis of modern medicine. The last category comprises some sixty

plants including foxgloves (*Digitalis*), yew (*Taxus*), snowdrops (specifically *Galanthus woronowii*) and Madagascar periwinkle (*Catharanthus roseus*).

The purpose of the RCP gardens, however, is not merely to show plants that are medically efficacious in some way. Unlike the Chelsea Physic Garden (see page 126), where the original aim was to provide examples of plants so that apothecaries could learn to recognize them, the RCP's garden is a horticultural lesson in the history of medicine.

If you take a tour of the garden – tours are offered on the first Wednesday of the month between March and October at 2 p.m. – you are likely to be disabused of any expectations regarding alternative remedies such as evening primrose (*Oenothera biennis*) and echinacea (*Echinacea angustifolia*). The plants are viewed through the prism of rigorous clinical research – there is no place here for myth, hearsay or superstition.

Dr Henry Oakeley, Garden Fellow at the RCP and a world expert on orchids, explained that it was only when the college moved to its current home in Regent's Park in 1965 that it was able at last to have any sort of garden at all. The emphasis is very much on its educational role, but at a casual glance you would see nothing museum-like about the gardens if you happened to stroll past.

The beds, most of which are organized according to their continents of origin, are set around Sir Denys Lasdun's

---

Photographs by Marianne Majerus

Opium poppies (*Papaver somniferum*) thrive in the gardens at the Royal College of Physicians in Regent's Park. Codeine is derived from this species.

modernist building, which forms an elegant counterpoint to the surrounding terrace by John Nash. You could be forgiven for thinking that the eight gardens in front of the houses in St Andrew's Place, opposite the main building, look like any other attractive, extremely well-maintained front gardens. In fact, they hold the plants used in the RCP's *Pharmacopoeia* of 1618, and they were designed by head gardener Jane Knowles.

Such a balance between a collection of plants that is of educational and historic interest, and a design that is pleasing aesthetically might appear difficult to achieve, but Knowles and her team make it look easy. Their feat is even more impressive when you learn that the soil in the front gardens of St Andrew's Place is only about 15 cm/6 inches deep in places; that there is no space whatsoever for raising or cosseting plants, apart from a tiny greenhouse; and that there is nowhere to have a compost heap or store all the kit that gardeners need.

Above left, above right and **left** The little front gardens of the Nash terrace opposite the main building contain the plants used in the RCP's *Pharmacopoeia* of 1618. They are grouped according to the part of the plant that is useful: petals, roots, leaves and so on.
Above According to tradition, the large plane tree has developed from a cutting taken from the tree below which the ancient Greek physician Hippocrates sat while teaching students.

> '**Many herbs were described as provoking lust - a claim that owed more to marketing strategy than scientific evidence.**'

LUST-PROVOKING HERBS

A tour of the garden begins in front of the RCP building, where the North American bed is situated. It continues with the St Andrew's Place gardens, where each garden is organized according to which part of the plant was used medicinally – flowers, roots, leaves and so on.

Inula, which is enjoying a resurgence in popularity thanks to the fashion for prairie-style planting, is represented here in the form of elecampane (*I. helenium*). According to Culpeper, it was good for the stomach, for coughs and shortness of breath, and it provoked lust. Dr Oakeley pointed out that many herbs were described as provoking lust – a claim that owed more to marketing strategy than to any scientific evidence.

At the end of St Andrew's Place, through the gates, is the Main Garden, which contains plants associated with the classical world, the arid-zone beds and plants from other continents. Here is *Acanthus dioscoridis*, named after Dioscorides, who was

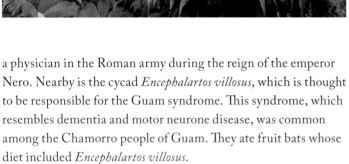

a physician in the Roman army during the reign of the emperor Nero. Nearby is the cycad *Encephalartos villosus*, which is thought to be responsible for the Guam syndrome. This syndrome, which resembles dementia and motor neurone disease, was common among the Chamorro people of Guam. They ate fruit bats whose diet included *Encephalartos villosus*.

For centuries, this sort of toxicity has given some plants a sort of sinister notoriety. Most of us know that deadly nightshade (*Atropa belladonna*) and yew are poisonous, and the infamous upas tree (*Antiaris toxicaria*) of Java – which was supposed to poison all animal life within a radius of 25 kilometres/15½ miles – was celebrated in literature by none other than Lord Byron and Charles Dickens.

As Dr Oakeley observed, nearly all plants are poisonous – they have to be, because they cannot get up and run away. Modern biochemists, however, see these characteristics slightly differently. Any plant that contains a substance that has the ability to inhibit cell growth, for example, arouses interest because it may have the potential to lead to a cancer cure.

From the point of view of a consultant physician like Dr Oakeley, more frightening than poisonous plants is the alacrity with which the general public will buy alternative remedies that are at best ineffective and, at worst, downright dangerous. He cited *Aristolochia clematitis*, whose use in

Chinese medicine has led to an epidemic of renal failures and kidney cancers in recent years.

DANGEROUS REMEDIES

Senokot, a product freely available over the counter as a laxative, is obtained from *Senna corymbosa*, which contains anthraquinones. These stimulate the nerve cells of the smooth muscle of the large bowel, which is what causes the purgative effect. However, with regular use, the bowel nerves can become permanently damaged, thus, said Dr Oakeley, causing the condition it treats to become permanent.

There is also no evidence – scientific or historic – to support the notion that the large plane tree (*Platanus orientalis* subsp. *insularis*) in the centre of the lawn at the RCP is related to the tree beneath which Hippocrates (*c.*460–*c.*370 BC) sat to teach his students on the Greek island of Kos. The RCP tree itself did at least come from Kos, and it is a handsome symbol of the history of medicine, so no one is complaining.

Behind it is a bed containing plants from the southern hemisphere, many of which have uses in muthi (traditional southern African) medicine. This bed sweeps round beneath the black wall of the Wolfson lecture theatre to the south-facing members' terrace, where an array of pots containing subtropical plants basks in the sunshine. These include brugmansia, a source

of scopolamine, which is used to treat irritable bowel syndrome, and lemon (*Citrus × limon*). Lemon was a cure for scurvy in the Royal Navy until the invention in 1867 of Rose's lime juice, a patented drink that preserved the vitamin C in the juice without the use of alcohol – hence the nickname 'Limeys'.

Continue walking around the lawn and you come to another cure for scurvy, in the flower bed that contains oriental plants, and more specimens from the southern hemisphere. Captain John Winter, whose ship, *Elizabeth*, was part of the flotilla that sailed with Captain Francis Drake in 1577 on the mission to circumnavigate the globe, discovered that soup made from the bark of *Drimys winteri* was anti-scorbutic, thus saving his crew.

We like to think that our own epoch is the one in which great medical breakthroughs have been made. It is humbling to remember that many of the cures have existed for centuries.

Opposite above left Plants from the southern hemisphere are also included in this medicinal collection.
Opposite above right Chinese foxglove (*Rehmannia elata*) is used somewhat controversially as a Chinese remedy for diabetes.
Above These white flowers belong to deadly poisonous *Aconitum napellus* subsp. *vulgare* 'Albidum'.
Right (clockwise from top left) *Leonurus cardiaca*; *Aristolochia clematitis*; *Aloe striatula* and the leaves of *Eucomis comosa* 'Sparkling Burgundy'; *Mandragora officinarum*.

A DESIGNER HARVEST

BUSHY PARK ALLOTMENTS, BUSHY PARK

For most allotment holders, Best in Show might mean a prize-winning marrow or a silver cup for their tomatoes or shallots. For Cleve West, however, Best in Show is the coveted RHS Chelsea Flower Show award he has achieved not just once but twice. Altogether he has been awarded seven RHS gold medals, and he is one of the most respected garden designers in Britain today.

At heart, though, you sense that West is happier pottering about in his allotment than rubbing shoulders with celebrities at prestigious garden shows. He is a modest man, who is not too embarrassed to recount his experiences with bindweed (*Convolvulus arvensis*) or to admit that his allotment shed – built with reclaimed material – was immediately christened 'The Wonky Shed' by his fellow allotmenteers at Bushy Park.

He says his first experience with vegetables came when he was sent on an errand by his mother to buy something from the DIY store, and potatoes from the supermarket. To his delight, he found that the DIY store – an old-fashioned hardware store – sold potatoes, and thus saved a trip to the supermarket.

Photographs by Hugo Rittson Thomas

The Wonky Shed, built with reclaimed wood, is one of the features of garden designer Cleve West's allotment in west London.

Returning home, he found himself the target of family humour. What kind of idiot bought seed potatoes (for that is what they were) instead of ordinary eating potatoes? The young West was defiant. What was wrong with them? Were they poisonous? No one seemed to be able to give him an answer, and the rejected tubers languished in the vegetable rack, inevitably producing shoots. West planted them to see what would happen and launched himself on a lifetime's fascination with growing plants.

ANCIENT MEASUREMENT

Allotments – known as Schrebergarten in Germany, or victory gardens in the United States – have been around in some form or other in England since Anglo-Saxon times, but it was only in 1908 that the Small Holdings and Allotments Act legally obliged local authorities to provide plots according to demand. In 1925, further legislation made it impossible for local authorities to sell off or convert allotments without government consent (which effectively means without a public inquiry).

Allotments are measured in rods, an ancient unit that dates back to Anglo-Saxon times. It is said to be the length of stick (rod) that was needed to control a team of eight oxen, harnessed in four pairs. A ten-rod allotment – about the size of a doubles tennis court – is generally considered enough land to provide food for a family, but many people find that a five-rod

allotment is less daunting, while still providing enough produce for a small household.

Over the years, allotments have gone in and out of fashion: during the Second World War, there was a huge rise in popularity, and again in the 1970s, thanks to the energy crises and the first stirrings of the self-sufficiency movement. When West took on his five-rod plot, in 1999, there was no such thing as waiting lists for allotments. Today, the popularity of the grow-your-own movement has seen a huge rise in waiting lists, especially in the inner cities.

The typical image of an allotmenteer is an elderly man in a flat cap and tweed jacket, but in reality there is no such person. In the cities, especially, allotments are multicultural communities and many plots may boast a wealth of exotic fruit and vegetables cared for by a multiplicity of nationalities.

West believes that the dynamics of allotment life depend on variety: 'Not just in terms of vegetables, methods or styles, but in the characters of the people. Each person has their own idiosyncratic ways – everyone is different.' At the same time, he says, the sense of community came as a huge shock:

I enjoy the solitude of gardening – it is what drew me to it as a career – but the allotment turned out to be challenging in a way I had not expected. People talked.

Not only that, but some people liked to talk quite a bit. You have to realize that this is part of the deal and learn to keep moving while talking if you are to get any work done at all. You also have to understand that some of the things you are being told may turn out to be pearls of wisdom.

As with all vegetable gardeners, for West and his partner Christine Eatwell growing your own leads inevitably to eating your own, and as soon as possible. They have built a pizza oven on site at their Bushy Park allotment, and their barbecues – not to mention West's onion bhaji recipe – are a favourite for birthdays and other family gatherings.

Christine has four grandchildren, all of whom have come to see the allotment as part of the fun of visiting grandma. For the younger ones, Florence and Otto, the plot seems a magical place, and West believes this experience helps build respect and passion for the natural world:

Unearthing new potatoes and getting them in the pot within minutes, or throwing freshly picked sweetcorn like an American football to the catcher at the grill is not only fun – it proves just how tasty fresh-picked food can be.

Opposite West says he finds the ramshackle process of recycling and improvising on an allotment very inspiring.
Top and **above** The plot is a sea of blossom and forget-me-nots in spring.
Right A gateway has here been given the designer treatment.

Below West's design for RHS Chelsea Flower Show 2014 was
inspired by ancient Persian paradise gardens.
Right The fountain was built from Bath limestone and flint.
Bottom West's plant palette included hesperis and cerinthe.

INSPIRATION FOR CREATIVITY

As one of the UK's foremost garden designers, West believes design has a place even on a shambolic allotment complete with wonky shed:

> What on earth has design got to do with growing food? The answer is: everything! How you arrange your plot, whether you draw it on paper or not, is design. You are arranging space either logically, intuitively or creatively to get the best from it in terms of production.

However, you do not need to have design training in order to express yourself on an allotment, West points out:

> The very ramshackle nature of recycling, improvising and modifying means the plot is inspiration for creativity. Decay in all its forms is more acceptable, and rotting wood, rusting metal, moss, lichen and fungi are not just the natural ingredients, they are the stars of the show.

Above Allotments may look messy and chaotic, but they are designed to produce the maximum crop within the space available.
Left There is sometimes a small corner for growing flowers, which add a cottage-garden charm to the utilitarian plots.

POWER TO THE PEOPLE

ECCLESTON SQUARE, PIMLICO

It is a safe bet that most of those who visit the Passport Office near Eccleston Square, a short walk from Victoria station, are unaware that the leafy gardens they can glimpse through the railings are the site of a glorious revolution.

At first glance, there is nothing to tell you that the garden contains anything out of the ordinary. There is no obvious evidence of the 150 roses (shrub and climbing), the 200 camellias, the 35 tree peonies and the 70 ceanothus. (Eccleston Square is home to one of the national collections of ceanothus.) Look a bit closer, however, and your attention may be caught by the Tarzan-bearing cables of a climbing rose scrambling up through the trees, or the wisteria that encircles a mature London plane (*Platanus × hispanica*). You may catch sight of the pale trunks of a grove of white Himalayan birches (*Betula utilis* var. *jacquemontii*) rising from a bed of *Smyrnium perfoliatum*, and realize that the guiding hands behind this 1.25-hectare/3-acre garden belong to some very knowledgeable plantspeople.

Eccleston Square was built by Thomas Cubitt, who began to develop South Belgravia (as he called what is now Pimlico) in

Photographs by Marianne Majerus

A wisteria grows around an ancient plane tree in the garden at Eccleston Square – its purple blossom blending with irises and lilac.

1825. Eccleston, Warwick and St George's squares contained some of the grandest houses, which were aimed at the well-to-do middle and upper-middle classes. Like many of the London squares, Eccleston Square was open only to residents. For a brief interlude during the First World War, however, it was used for training – a photograph from 1918 shows policewomen on parade on the lawn. Apart from this, life continued uneventfully – perhaps too uneventfully, for in 1981 the residents rose up in protest about the maintenance of the gardens, which they felt were becoming neglected. They sacked the garden committee and organized a work party of volunteers to clear the rubbish that had accumulated. One group of neighbours even set fire to the scruffy collection of sheds.

CAR PARK THREAT

One of the residents of Eccleston Square was Roger Phillips, the botanist and photographer, who with Martyn Rix is author of *The Botanical Garden*. He was persuaded to take charge of the improvements, which was just as well because six years later, in 1987, the then freeholder decided that it would be a good idea to build an underground car park beneath the square. This would have necessitated the removal of many of the mature trees, and ensured that the square itself would have been subject to the comings and goings of countless motorists.

As Todd Longstaffe-Gowan points out in his book, *The London Square*, the growth of traffic in the capital after the Second World War put many London squares at risk. Although such plans faced vociferous protests as early as the 1950s, Finsbury Square, Cavendish Square, Bloomsbury Square and Cadogan Place Gardens (see page 196) all eventually fell victim to this trend. Fortunately, the local authority (Westminster City Council) refused planning permission at Eccleston Square, and in 1988 the residents were able to buy the freehold.

In *The 3,000-Mile Garden*, published in 1997 to accompany a Channel 4 series of the same name, Phillips described the work of restoring the garden in his correspondence with the American food writer Leslie Land. His book was a sort of horticultural version of Helene Hanff's *84, Charing Cross Road*. In January 2010, Phillips was awarded the MBE for services to London's garden squares.

In the Great Storm of 1987 hurricane-force winds brought down trees that had stood for hundreds of years across the south of England during one wild October night. Eccleston Square lost seventeen trees, including seven of the original London planes. The loss of a huge London plane may dismay people, but there is no doubt that the 1987 storm had the beneficial effect of opening up gardens and allowing in more light – without letting in the developers. Although London squares – indeed,

London gardens – may benefit from the presence of mature trees, it means gardeners have to cope with areas of dry shade.

SUBTROPICAL SPECIMENS

One of the first things Phillips did when he took over the supervision of the Eccleston Square gardens was to import tonnes of spent hops from the Young's brewery across the river in Wandsworth, which provided organic matter to enrich the soil. The soil is reasonably free-draining, which explains why the more subtropical specimens survive without too much trouble.

Dahlias and agapanthus flourish in the sunnier borders, while echiums seem determined to compete with towering cordylines in a 'how high can I go?' competition. The dry shade beneath the trees has healthy colonies of liriope and *Geranium endressii*. Tennis courts at the Victoria end of the garden are screened by climbers, and a very attractive greenhouse, painted dark green, has taken the place of the scruffy old sheds.

Above The flowering shrubs make a magnificent display.
Opposite (clockwise from top) A smart greenhouse provides winter shelter for more tender specimens; Himalayan birches have been underplanted with *Smyrnium perfoliatum*; golden wallflowers complement the yellow blooms of *Rosa banksiae* 'Lutea'; one of the enormous plane trees frames a view of Westminster Cathedral.

Ball games are prohibited, apart from cricket which must be played with a soft ball. Bikes and trikes are banned too. So is music – radios, CD players, musical instruments and so on – although residents are allowed to use the barbecue area, which is bricked for this purpose.

These rules might sound draconian, but they ensure peace and quiet for everyone who wants to use the gardens. During the week, this tends to be older people and mothers with young children, and on a summer weekend, if the weather is good, the lawn is as busy as Brighton beach, says Neville Capil, who has been head gardener since 2005. Each summer, there is a barbecue party for all residents, keyholders and their guests, with wine supplied by the residents' association.

Capil, a New Zealander, is as much of a plantaholic as Phillips himself, particularly when it comes to plants from the southern hemisphere. He is responsible for the presence

Top left, **centre left**, **bottom left** and **left** This entrance to the garden is framed by a pergola, over which scramble roses and wisteria. The structure gives a sense of intimacy to this central London garden, just minutes from Victoria station.
Above Eccleston Square holds a National Collection of ceanothus, which includes more than seventy different species and cultivars. There are also 200 different camellias.

'Roger Phillips, the botanist and a resident of the square, was persuaded to take charge of the improvements.'

of a kauri pine (*Agathis australis*), which can grow to 50 m/164 ft, the New Zealand Christmas tree (*Metrosideros excelsa*) and the white sunflower tree (*Rojasianthe superba*), which grows in the highlands of central America but seems to find central London an acceptable alternative.

There is no cosseting of plants here; roses are planted with mycorrhizal fungi to get them off to a good start, and given a feed of poultry manure after the first year, but there is no spraying to get rid of blackspot. Leafmould, produced in abundance with so many big trees around, is used as a mulch, which means the gardens really look after themselves.

As you might expect, with an organic approach, and this number of flowering plants, the wildlife in the garden is thriving. There are bat boxes and even a barn owl box. Human visitors can see the square on the National Gardens Scheme open day, which usually takes place in mid-May, or on Sunday afternoon during the Open Garden Squares Weekend, which is mid-June.

PAINTING WITH PLANTS

ST REGIS CLOSE, MUSWELL HILL

We are told that dogs tend to look like their owners, but what about gardens? It is a thought that crosses your mind when you visit the Muswell Hill garden of Susan Bennett and Earl Hyde. It is crammed with visual jokes, cultural references and clever allusions, such as the Psycho shed, with its decorative ironwork, or the Forbidden City, with its turquoise ceramic eaves. Their garden in St Regis Close is colourful, original, positive and creative – just like Bennett and Hyde.

The first thing you see as you step into the garden is a chimney piece, painted a brilliant green and red. On it sits an ormolu clock, flanked by two brass candle sconces, while a fiery melange of colours – red and yellow tulips in spring, for example, or copper heucheras and scarlet busy Lizzies in autumn – blazes in the grate.

The fireplace 'came from a neighbour's house', and as you make your way around the garden these words become a familiar refrain. The plywood for the shed? It came from a neighbour who had bought it for a DIY job he never got around to doing. The candelabra in the temple? From Italian neighbours who were

---

Photographs by Marianne Majerus

One of the two ponds at St Regis Close. Vibrant colours, such as the vivid scarlet of the tulips, are characteristic of this garden.

moving. The little stained glass window? From a church that was being demolished at the top of the road. What about the panels, painted a brilliant Chinese yellow, that form the backdrop for Liberace Terrace? The remains of yet another neighbour's garage roof, damaged by police officers who ran across it while chasing a burglar.

Then there is the group of metal chairs and table outside the conservatory, all of which have been painted dark green with flashes of bright red and gold. The 'stand' for the hanging baskets is an old wrought-iron standard lamp, while the table came out of a skip, where it had been discarded by some Greek Cypriot neighbours.

HARMONIOUS PARTNERSHIP

What does not come out of a skip cost only a few pence. The plastic cladding that forms the circular base of the temple dome is from a DIY store. What looks like ironwork along the wall of Liberace Terrace, and which decorates the Psycho shed, are sections of faux-Victorian plastic garden fencing from a local pound shop.

The Psycho shed is inspired by the American thriller television series *Bates Motel*, which itself was modelled on a painting by Edward Hopper entitled *The House by the Railroad*. It is typical of the St Regis Close garden as a whole: this is not

'The garden is crammed with visual jokes, cultural references and clever allusions, such as the Psycho shed.'

just a lot of old junk slung together, but the product of two creative minds working in harmony.

Some of the ideas may not yet be realized – such as the spiral staircase destined to twine up an old apple tree – but others are put into action with an attention to detail that is only to be expected from people who make their living from art.

BUST OF BEETHOVEN
Bennett and Hyde are studio potters (the studio is at the centre of the garden). Hyde makes architectural models and figurines, as well as beautiful garden pots inspired by sea urchin shells, while Bennett creates a range of pottery candleholders and incense burners. They also specialize in individually designed commemorative mugs and plaques, which are popular with West End actors. In fact, it was Maureen Lipman who first brought their garden to public attention when she mentioned it during a newspaper interview, after she had come to order one of

Opposite Materials for the temple (top) came from a DIY shop, while the 'ironwork' on the Psycho shed (left) is plastic, faux-Victorian garden edging from a bargain store.

Top *Tulipa* 'Queen of Sheba', *Tulipa* 'Apeldoorn's Elite' and *Tulipa* 'Jan Reus' are complemented by forget-me-nots and *Viburnum × burkwoodii*.

Above The yellow wall of Liberace Terrace, named after the flamboyant pianist, contrasts with the bright purple of a clematis.

Right This stained-glass window, which was salvaged from a local church that was being demolished, has been set into new brickwork.

Top A Chinese-style trellis with turquoise ceramic 'eaves' screens the potting and greenhouse area, nicknamed the 'Forbidden City'.
Above A painted mangle houses terracotta heads.
Left Within the painted fireplace are glowing flame-like colours.
Opposite The miniature pagoda was made by Hyde.

their mugs for a colleague. As a result, Bennett was contacted by the National Gardens Scheme (NGS) and persuaded to open to the public; she is now an assistant county organizer for the NGS.

Hyde's work is used extensively throughout the garden. The ormolu clock on the chimney piece is his; it is inspired by the After Eight chocolates logo. There is a miniature Orthodox cathedral by the pond nearest the house, where Hyde felt the corner needed brightening up. He marbled the columns of the temple and sculpted the busts of Beethoven and Liberace, which will sit each end of Liberace Terrace. Inside the temple is the figure of an Indian dancer. Bennett has christened her Maud ('because she came into the garden') Lakshmi de Medici.

ORIENTAL AMBIENCE

When Bennett first moved into her house in 1966, the garden was a fraction of its present size – a conventional plot running parallel to those on either side. Behind these gardens, however, was a strip of land owned by the Home Office, which was persuaded to sell it. For a while, the couple shared it with a neighbour, but now own it all.

At the far end of the L-shaped garden is a pond and a mirrored gateway that gives the impression of the plot stretching on beyond the boundary. Even the keyhole has a piece of mirror behind it so as not to spoil the illusion. At the base of the gateway

are a collection of clay heads, self-portraits made by pupils at North London Collegiate, the independent girls' school, where Bennett used to teach art.

There is an oriental ambience at this end of the garden, with bamboo and red trellis forming a backdrop to the vibrant autumn foliage of acers and Virginia creeper (*Parthenocissus quinquefolia*). Hyde has developed this theme with the 'Forbidden City', which is Bennett's greenhouse and potting area. Hyde made the vibrant turquoise eave tiles, but the greenhouse, which is bright red, is from Hartley Botanic.

All these ideas are so intriguing that it is quite easy to be distracted from the planting. This is vivid and strong, and more than holds its own against the dramatic backdrops. In late spring, there are wallflowers (*Erysimum*), ceanothus and tulips (including bi-coloured varieties such as *Tulipa* 'Judith Leyster' and *T.* 'Abu Hassan', which give way to dahlias, cosmos, begonias and lilies in midsummer.

Around the shed, there is a greener, more woodland feel, with aquilegias and hostas in the shade of a willow tree (*Salix*), while around the koi pond there are grasses and the cool, white spathes of *Zantedeschia aethiopica*.

So if this is what the garden looks like, what about the dog? Well, the couple have a Weimaraner called Phoebe, and she comes in a subtle shade of grey.

MEDICINE FOR THE SOUL

CHELSEA PHYSIC GARDEN, CHELSEA

The ornate gates of the Chelsea Physic Garden carry the arms of the Worshipful Society of Apothecaries, who founded the garden in 1673. They depict Apollo, the Greek god of healing, killing the serpent Python, which represents disease. The gates open on to the Chelsea Embankment, but they are not used by the public. They are only opened on two occasions: when a member of the royal family comes to visit, and when the manure is delivered – not on the same day, one hopes.

The Chelsea Physic Garden is often described as one of London's garden oases. It covers 1.6 hectares/4 acres, and it is just along the road from the grounds of the Royal Hospital, where RHS Chelsea Flower Show is held every year.

The Society of Apothecaries is one of the big London guilds. Their Livery Hall has been at Blackfriars, in the City of London, since 1632, and, until 1922, they manufactured and sold pharmaceutical products there. However, the Society decided that it needed to rent somewhere in which to grow plants for its apprentices to study and learn to identify.

Photographs by Marianne Majerus

A statue of Sir Hans Sloane commemorates the Royal Physician who in 1722 leased the physic garden to the Society of Apothecaries for £5 a year in perpetuity.

The Chelsea site was perfect. The river access was crucial, as plants, seeds, supplies and so on could be transported by water, which at that time was safer and quicker than travelling by road. By 1722, the freehold had been acquired by Sir Hans Sloane, the Royal Physician, who leased it to the Society at a peppercorn rent.

When we ordinary gardeners build a pond, we go to the DIY store or the garden centre to buy hard landscaping materials. When the Chelsea Physic Garden built the ornamental pond next to the statue of Sir Hans Sloane, it used the basaltic lava that had served as ballast in the ship which took Sir Joseph Banks on a voyage to Iceland in 1772. It was dropped off at the Physic Garden when the ship arrived back in London.

The pieces of carved stone around the pond look as if they are from an architectural salvage yard. In a sense they are: they once formed part of the Tower of London.

COSMETICS AND PERFUME

The Chelsea Physic Garden was originally divided into four, and until recently this was still pretty much the case. One section was devoted to medicine; one to the botanical order beds, arranged by families of plants; one to the great plant hunters and their discoveries; and one to woodland plants, such as bamboo.

This last section, at the river end, was revamped by head gardener Nick Bailey when he arrived in 2010. Called the Garden of Edible and Useful Plants, it opened officially in May 2012, and anything that is used to make paper, or rope, or dye, or fabric can be found here. The area works very well, not only from an aesthetic point of view but also as a way of displaying plants. It still looks like a garden, rather than a classroom. There is a perfumery amphitheatre, full of fragrant plants, and beds dedicated to hygiene and cosmetics. In the Edible Garden, there is a herb, spice and flavourings bed, a viticulture collection and a space dedicated to heritage vegetables. Beekeepers may be interested in the bee forage beds (the Physic Garden has its own hives), which contain *Erysimum* 'Bowles's Mauve' and other pollinator favourites. There is still a thicket of bamboo, a testament to its role as the world's most useful plant. Bamboo is used for construction (both housing and agricultural), textiles, paper, charcoal, furniture, bedding, medicine and instruments, as well as a food.

Top left The order beds display different botanical families.
Far left Agave grows alongside chilli peppers and fennel.
Centre left The pond is situated near the statue of Sir Hans Sloane.
Bottom left The Garden of Edible and Useful Plants includes plants used for fabric and rope as well as herbs and vegetables.
Above The design of the Edible Garden is inspired by eighteenth-century potagers, and the paths are made from traditional clay bricks.

'The pieces of carved stone around the pond were brought from the Tower of London.'

WARM MICROCLIMATE

The whole garden faces south, and this, combined with the protection afforded by the surrounding buildings, creates a warm microclimate. If you take a guided tour (highly recommended), you will probably be told that the Chelsea Physic Garden can be up to 7°C/12°F warmer than the surrounding streets – and London itself is an urban heat island. In recent years, the lowest minimum air temperature recorded has been 1.27°C/34°F. This means that otherwise tender plants, such as *Geranium maderense* or the towering echiums, can flourish without fear of being cut down by freezing temperatures (although a fleece tent is erected over them every winter just in case).

The trees are superb specimens, and include cork oak (*Quercus suber*), maidenhair tree (*Ginkgo*), mulberry (*Morus*) and yew (*Taxus*). Yew is such a familiar tree in British churchyards and gardens that it is difficult to imagine a time when it was scarce. However, the English cut down so many yews to make

longbows during the Middle Ages that at one point England was in danger of running out of yew trees altogether.

For many gardeners, the most eye-catching exhibits as you enter the Chelsea Physic Garden are the botanical order beds, with their billowing perennials and colourful flowers. Many of the most fascinating plants, however, are to be found in the medicinal section. There is *Veratrum viride*, for example, a highly toxic herbaceous perennial used by some Native American tribes to elect a new leader. All the candidates would eat a leaf, and the last one to vomit was made chief. Perhaps they should adopt this method for the US elections. It would be much cheaper than months of campaigning – and far more entertaining.

Then there is Madagascar periwinkle (*Catharanthus roseus*), a synthetic version of which is used in the treatment of leukaemia and lymphoma. It contains alkaloids in its sap – interestingly, one of the side effects of treatment is hair loss, just as with chemotherapy.

The Robert Fortune tank pond, a popular part of the garden with visiting schoolchildren in search of tadpoles or newts, is named after the Scottish botanist who was curator at the Physic Garden from 1846 to 1848. Together with John Lindley, Fortune improved the state of the gardens and the collections, but he is more famous as the man who helped develop Assam as a major tea-planting region.

FERN FEVER

The Cool Fernery, a small greenhouse on the west side of the Chelsea Physic Garden, is a restored version of the 1862 original, built according to a design developed by Nathaniel Bagshaw Ward for the collection of ferns and aquatic and bog plants. Ward is better known as the inventor of the Wardian case, the sealed glass case that in the second half of the nineteenth century enabled plant hunters to ship living plants home from abroad. Fortune established his tea plantations by using Wardian cases to smuggle 20,000 tea plants to India from Shanghai, China. The majority of fern varieties housed in the Cool Fernery are natives or cultivars first described by Thomas Moore. He was curator between 1848 and 1887, when the passion for collecting ferns – known as pteridomania, or fern-fever – was at its height.

In 1679, 1,200 different plants were recorded at the Physic Garden. Today, there are 5,000 taxa, and the intervening 350 years have seen huge leaps in our knowledge of botany, of medicine and of the way plants can be used in our everyday lives. It is a very impressive record for such a tranquil spot.

Above Spires of mullein (*Verbascum*) soar up in front of the Perfumery Amphitheatre. Dried mullein leaves and stems were once used to make lamp wicks, while tea from mullein leaves was also a remedy for coughs. Alternatives to tobacco often contain mullein.

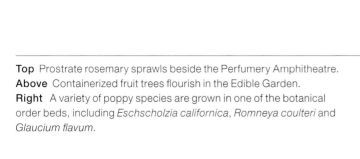

Top Prostrate rosemary sprawls beside the Perfumery Amphitheatre.
Above Containerized fruit trees flourish in the Edible Garden.
Right A variety of poppy species are grown in one of the botanical order beds, including *Eschscholzia californica*, *Romneya coulteri* and *Glaucium flavum*.

Top Benches line the path beneath a magnificent specimen of *Rosa brunonii*. This rare species is native to Afghanistan and Pakistan. **Above** and **right** (clockwise from above) Cardoon and chicory; *Cucurbita maxima* 'Uchiki Kuri'; buckwheat; chilli pepper; *Calandrinia grandiflora*.

CHAPTER FOUR
HIGH-RISE RETREATS

ROOM AT THE TOP

HENRIETTA STREET, COVENT GARDEN

When Amir Schlezinger was commissioned to design the roof terrace at Henrietta Street, in the heart of Covent Garden, it was late spring of 2012, and London was convulsed by feverish preparations for the Olympic Games.

On paper, his commission was an exciting one. The roof terrace was unusually large, with 360-degree views of the London skyline, and its owners were young and enthusiastic. Schlezinger came up with a design that split the terrace into three sections, delineated by broad, shallow steps: a central social area, with an impressive outside kitchen and massive rotisserie; a tiled area that catches the morning sun and forms an outdoor breakfast room; and an area laid with artificial grass.

Most of Schlezinger's clients work all day, he points out, so a network of outdoor lighting – uplighters for the trees, downlighters for the doors and barbecue area, and LEDs on the steps – as well as the addition of speakers mean that it is a great space in which to cook, listen to music and chill out.

Focal points – mainly architectural plants such as cordylines – lead the eye through the garden, while containers filled with

lavender (*Lavandula*), bergenia, euphorbia and libertia add scent and evergreen texture.

CLASSIC PROBLEMS

The logistical planning behind the creation of this urban eyrie is worthy of the best Hollywood heist plot. First, the roof needed to be resealed, which meant scaffolding had to be erected all around the building. Then came the classic problem facing any roof terrace builder – how to get the rubbish out, and the new building materials in. Schlezinger estimated that there were 10 tonnes of stuff to come down, and 20 tonnes of materials to go up. For this job, he decided to use a friend's mini-crane, which is like a pick-up truck with a hydraulic pump that can raise the crane to a height of 20 m/66 ft.

Henrietta Street is a busy, narrow one-way street, and there were only two parking bays from which the crane on the truck could operate. In addition, they needed an adjacent parking space in which to stack the building materials.

You need permission from the local authority to suspend the parking bays, and in the Henrietta Street area you can carry out this sort of manoeuvre only between 8 and 11 a.m.

Stuff coming down from the roof had to be put on to 'wait and load' skips, where the skip lorry arrives, stops in the middle of the street, loads up and takes the skip away again. As far as the

---

Photographs by Marianne Majerus

The roof terrace at Henrietta Street offers 360-degree views of the London skyline. Outdoor lighting allows the owners to enjoy the garden at night.

new materials – compost, pebbles, decking, tiles, planters and so on – were concerned, there was not enough time to load them all in one day, so some had to be left on the street overnight. Schlezinger went home that evening, he recalls, and had a very bad night's sleep.

Today, he shrugs it off as being part of the job. In London, being a permanent building site, the battle for anyone in the construction industry is to get access to the site, to get the materials to where you need them and to get on with the work. For example, while doing a roof terrace at Butler's Wharf, effectively a gated complex, Schlezinger found that vans were allowed access only after 11 a.m. Work finally got under way, until Saturday, when the power cut out at noon. It was the concierge's quiet way of telling them that no building work was allowed at weekends from Saturday midday until Monday morning.

One of Schlezinger's first projects included 2.5-m/8-ft olive trees weighing half a tonne, which had to be squeezed into the passenger lift. You learn lessons from these experiences, he says: 'Know your timetable and always carry a tape measure.'

Because of the fast-moving nature of London's population and property market, Schlezinger rarely sees a garden again after he has built it. 'The longest any of my clients has had a garden is twelve years,' said Schlezinger. 'Some 50 to 60 per cent of them are sold before I can have another look.'

DESIGN TRAINING

Schlezinger was born in Israel. His name, Amir, may sound Arabic, but it is Hebrew for 'treetop' or the 'upper branches of a tree'. In other words, the elite. His father was a keen gardener, but the young Amir's initial ambition was to be a drummer. However, in 1997, he enrolled at Capel Manor to study under Hilary Thomas, then head of the school of garden design, who had trained with John Brookes. Schlezinger loved the course, but when he graduated in June 2000 he had no idea what he was going to do.

He woke up one morning and the name 'mylandscapes' popped into his head. He decided to set up his own design practice, but no sooner did he start to get this under way than the events of 11 September 2001 threw the world into confusion. Ironically, his first commission came from a Pakistani Muslim.

TOUGH SPECIMENS

Roof terraces have their advantages aesthetically – the light changes every minute, and you have a dramatic big-sky backdrop

Above The central part of the roof terrace is decked, and is designed like an open-plan living room, with low seating and a kitchen.
Above right Plants play dual roles as focal points and windbreaks.
Right The kitchen area includes a large barbecue.

Top Two loungers set on an artificial lawn provide somewhere to relax
and read in this rooftop garden.
Above The breakfast area has white paving to make the most of the light.
Centre left and **left** Favourite plants include cordylines and bergenia.
Opposite The grey, powder-coated steel containers were designed
by Schlezinger to offer maximum stability and minimal loss of moisture.

– but they provide a tough environment for the plants themselves. The first problem is wind, for without the shelter of mature trees container plants are buffeted by the strange eddies and vortexes that occur between high buildings. Second, the reflected heat from hard surfaces, such as roofs and windows, can generate a warmer microclimate, which means pots dry out more quickly.

Schlezinger, like any designer, has his favourite plants, but the choice is more about what works than any personal preferences. He likes architectural plants that need little pruning, as they save on maintenance. However, he also favours deciduous trees, particularly those with coloured or flaking bark, such as Tibetan cherry (*Prunus serrula*), paper-bark maple (*Acer griseum*), white Himalayan birches (*Betula utilis* var. *jacquemontii*) and strawberry tree (*Arbutus unedo*). Cordylines are an obvious choice for a roof garden; they actively enjoy a hot,

dry climate – they hate sitting in cold, wet soil – and can be tied up in winter to prevent frost and wind damage. Chusan palm (*Trachycarpus fortunei*) looks even more exotic, but is very hardy, even in containers, as are olive trees (*Olea*).

Ilex crenata can be clipped or pruned just like box (*Buxus*), while lavender (*Lavandula*) is both drought-tolerant and fragrant. *Bergenia cordifolia* gives the impression of lush planting, while rustling bamboo – neatly clipped to leave the stems bare – helps provide white noise to mask the sound of traffic.

BESPOKE CONTAINERS

For the Henrietta Street roof terrace, as for all his gardens, Schlezinger designs his own containers. These are made of powder-coated steel, and form a tapered square, 80 degrees from the vertical, which can be put on castors. The crucial bit is the top. It has a cut-out section in the middle where the plant or the trunk comes through, but the fact that it is partially covered helps keep in moisture and keep out weeds. His containers come in two different shades of grey, to emphasize perspective.

Schlezinger does not attend trade shows and he has never designed a garden for the RHS Chelsea Flower Show. Most of his clients, he said, find him on Google. Alternatively, if you are passing an upmarket apartment block, keep an eye out for the man with the winch and the £1,200 mature olive tree.

'The logistical planning behind the creation of this urban eyrie is worthy of the best Hollywood heist plot.'

IRISES ON HIGH

CORSICA STREET, ISLINGTON

Professor Tim Macklem's roof terrace in north London, just a few hundred metres from the busy intersection that is Highbury corner, is a modern garden in every sense of the word. Its strong design is by Christopher Bradley-Hole, one of Britain's most distinguished garden designers, and recipient of three gold medals and Best Garden award at the RHS Chelsea Flower Show.

However, if Macklem's roof terrace conjures up an image of an expensive plot atop an academic's ivory tower, then think again. Macklem has built quite a bit of this garden himself, under the aesthetic direction of Bradley-Hole and with the help of a builder friend who appears to specialize in what can only be described as extreme gardening techniques.

Macklem and his partner, Gail Thorson, are from Canada – Ontario, to be precise. When they first moved into Corsica Street, the entire roof of their apartment was a terrace. The only plant material to speak of was a plane tree (*Platanus*)

Photographs by Marianne Majerus

Left The Corsica Street roof terrace houses a collection of bearded irises and is designed to offer light, privacy and glorious views.
Following pages An aluminium table and chairs on the cedar deck echo the metal containers in which grow ornamental grasses and irises.

in a container. One of the first things they did was to plant *Pinus parviflora* around the edge, because it reminded them of their native Canada, and the Great Lakes area.

INSPIRED BY VIRGIL

One evening in 1997, they were watching coverage of the RHS Chelsea Flower Show on television and noticed Bradley-Hole's Latin Garden, which was inspired by the life of the Roman poet Virgil. It was described by landscape critic Tim Richardson as 'probably the best Chelsea show garden in recent memory – perhaps the best garden ever seen at Chelsea'. The garden illustrated the three stages of Virgil's life, from his country childhood (he was the son of a rich landowner); through his rise to fame as a friend of the Emperor Augustus (the two were classmates at the Academy of Epidius in Rome); and his return to the rural life he loved and which inspired such works as the *Eclogues* and the *Georgics*. Anyone who saw this Latin Garden remembers it for its sense of place, for its unashamedly intellectual approach and for the magnificent, purple bearded irises and alliums.

Thorson's father had been a keen iris grower in the 1950s, and she and Macklem were captivated by Bradley-Hole's Latin Garden. 'We said, "that is it, that is the sort of garden we want",' remembered Macklem. 'I then looked Christopher Bradley-Hole

up in the phone book and asked him if he would come round and design our roof garden.'

Bradley-Hole agreed to do the design, and Macklem decided that he would do most of the work, in order to keep costs down:

> We wanted a garden we could look after, we did not want a low-maintenance arrangement. We had the pine trees already, and Christopher was happy for us to keep those. A friend and I built the deck, and we brought up all the soil and gravel ourselves.

IRIS COLLECTION

The Corsica Street roof terrace faces south, so the usual window-box style containers that you buy at a garden centre would have been too small to sustain plants year in, year out, even if a drip-feed irrigation system was installed. Bradley-Hole therefore introduced galvanized feed or stock troughs as planters, which were not only big but also gave a clean-cut modernist feel.

Macklem uses two of these planters for garden storage, and has cut lengths of ply which double as covers, or benches. Before studying law he trained as a linotype operator, and he obviously enjoys using his hands in the garden: the modernist washing line, with high-tensile wire running between two immaculately vertical, stainless steel poles is his work too.

The planting is straightforward and unfussy. As you would expect, there are lots of bearded irises – *I*. 'Bruno', *I*. 'Rosy Wings', *I*. 'Great Lakes', *I*. 'Jean Cayeux', *I*. 'Indian Chief', *I*. 'Chivalry', *I*. 'Happy Birthday' and *I*. 'Blue Rhythm', to name just a few. Originally, there were twenty-five varieties, but now there are around fifteen. Many of them are North American-bred, and were ordered mainly from two American nurseries – Superstition Iris Gardens in California and Winterberry Gardens in Virginia, both of whom specialize in historic irises and who will ship to the UK.

Bearded irises have changed a lot since the 1950s, says Macklem, and today's varieties are more exaggerated than the sort that Thorson's father used to grow: 'They are more ruffled, and the falls [the lower petals] are more horizontal than the traditional bearded irises.'

Irises, of course, bloom only for about six weeks, towards the end of spring, yet the garden still looks good in late summer, partly because of the architectural iris foliage. The pines provide an evergreen screen, and there are tall grasses planted

Above The deck was built by owner Tim Macklem.
Top right, centre right, right and **far right** The bearded irises are in bloom for only six weeks of the year, so an evergreen framework is provided by box topiary and pines, all grown in containers.

in containers at the east end of the terrace. Although these are deciduous – and include *Miscanthus sinensis* 'Graziella', *M.s.* 'Morning Light', *M. nepalensis* and *Calamagrostis × acutiflora* 'Karl Foerster' – the stems are tough enough to tolerate winter rain and wind, and the faded flower heads look wonderful with the low winter sun shining through them. If you cut down the ornamental grasses in early spring, just as they start into growth again, there will only be a few weeks when they are without foliage.

The other ingredients are a handsome olive (*Olea*) tree at the west end of the terrace, as well as annuals and perennials, such as cosmos and helenium, which are also grown in containers. Macklem said he and Thorson originally wanted to put the olive in the middle of the terrace, but Bradley-Hole had persuaded them to put it in the west corner. An unforeseen benefit is that it now masks next door's newly installed solar panels.

Above The garden was designed by Chelsea gold-medal winner Christopher Bradley-Hole, who chose the blue for the painted wall.
Left There are around fifteen varieties of bearded iris, many of which came from two specialist American nurseries.
Opposite Grasses such as *Panicum virgatum* 'Shenandoah' and *Miscanthus sinensis* 'Graziella' provide movement and colour.

ROOM AT THE TOP

The Corsica Street building itself, unlike the neighbouring brick terraces, is an old warehouse. The view from the roof is wonderful: looking out over the surrounding houses you can see the Shard, the Post Office Tower, the London Eye, the Gherkin, and, most appropriately, Canada Tower at Canary Wharf. St Paul's Cathedral is visible only in winter – in summer, it is hidden by trees.

In 2009, Macklem and Thorson decided that they wanted to build another room on the top of the house. They asked Bradley-Hole – who is a qualified architect – if he thought this would spoil the design of the roof terrace, but he liked the idea. He agreed to work out a volume for the room which would fit with the existing proportions. 'He has a strong sense of the kind of space he wants to achieve, and a perfect comprehension of space and light,' says Macklem.

'Many of the bearded irises are from two American nurseries that specialize in historic varieties.'

Some of the decking – made of imported clear cedar (that is, no knots) – had to be taken up to accommodate the new extension, and Macklem, an indefatigable recycler, was keen to reuse it. Bradley-Hole therefore suggested making a stepped catwalk to the stairs that lead down to the apartment. The western wall, which was originally yellow, was changed to blue. The new room allows even more use of the roof terrace, since it is a great place to sit on a winter afternoon.

Although a lift takes you to the apartment below, there is no other lift in the block so all the materials had to be brought up the stairs. How did they manage to bring up the olive tree and the beautiful, cloud-pruned cryptomeria? 'A friend who is a builder came up with the idea of wrapping some packing around the parapet at the front of the building,' explains Macklem. 'He fitted an electric winch and hauled the trees up using one of those tonne bags that aggregates come in.'

Even more impressive was the builder's technique when the pine trees needed repotting – four of them were getting on for 1.75 m/6 ft high. According to Macklem: 'He worked out that they would be pretty much pot-bound in their old containers. So he craned them up into the air, and then whacked the old containers with a crowbar. They fell off, leaving the root ball intact.' As Virgil put it, in Book 10 of the *Aeneid*, 'Audentis Fortuna iuvat' (Fortune favours the brave).

PINNACLE OF PERFECTION

COUTTS SKYLINE GARDEN, CHARING CROSS

I do not think it was the view of Nelson's Column, or the blue sky above, that made the raspberries on the Coutts roof garden taste so good. The blackberries were delicious too – as were the fennel, the sorrel, the peas and the tomatoes.

High above the Strand perches a gourmet paradise for one of Britain's oldest banks. Each of the four sides of the Coutts London headquarters boasts its own plot: Kitchen Garden, Herb (or Meadow) Garden, Fruit Garden and Cottage Garden.

This is not the sort of roof terrace where you sit and bask in the sun. It is strictly a production line – with the emphasis on line. It is only the width of the average office desk, although each side is about 20 m/66 ft long.

The roof garden has two functions: first, to grow amazing produce for the chef; and, second, to provide a green environment that will attract pollinators. The garden was the creation of Richard Vine, a talented and dedicated garden designer (who sadly died in autumn 2014) who established the garden to work on so many different levels.

Photographs by Marianne Majerus

A narrow parapet around the Coutts headquarters provides four different growing areas high above Charing Cross station.

For the Coutts kitchens, led by chef Peter Fiori, the emphasis is on taste, variety and freshness. The guiding principle is what the Italians call saltimbocca – something so fresh that it 'jumps into the mouth'. Thus, there is not just one variety of mint (*Mentha*), but many – even Peruvian black mint, also known as Mexican marigold, and not really a mint at all. It is a member of the *Tagetes* genus (its botanical name is *T. minuta*), which explains its feathery leaves; like mint, it can be used to make a herbal tea that is good for colds and respiratory ailments. Anyone plagued by bindweed (*Convolvulus arvensis*) or ground elder (*Aegopodium podagraria*) might like to note that Peruvian black mint has a reputation for clearing the ground around of perennial weeds.

The Herb (or Meadow) Garden looks west, across the back of St Martin-in-the-Fields, and it is a perfect spot to grow Mediterranean herbs such as lavender (*Lavandula*) and rosemary (*Rosmarinus*), which can bask in sunshine uninterrupted by neighbouring high buildings. On one side of the terrace is a hand rail, and on the other is a mansard roof, which gets baking hot on a sunny day – hot enough to burn your arm if you absent-mindedly lean against it.

In the Kitchen Garden, which faces the dome of the Coliseum, containers of taller plants, such as runner beans, are set back into the window recesses to stop them getting knocked over by the wind. A grapevine – Pinot Meunier – curls its way

along the hand rail, which makes a good substitute for a vertical support. From early autumn onwards, this is a shadier garden compared to the other three, but in high summer containers laden with tomatoes, such as 'San Marzano' or 'Sun Gold' ripen fast along the hand rail. There is a crop rotation system, and once one vegetable has gone over it is ruthlessly ripped out and something else goes in its place.

The Fruit Garden is the hottest garden. It faces south, and has a view of Charing Cross station. Interestingly, raspberries, which might be expected to prefer less intense heat and a bit more moisture in the air, produce succulent fruit here. Thriving are red and golden raspberries, as well as cultivated blackberries, which are equally as delicious. The only fruit that does not seem to like this rooftop perch are gooseberries, which ironically are supposed to like lots of sun.

Left The Herb Garden faces the church of St Martin-in-the-Fields. Nearly every part of the garden offers a view of Nelson's Column, just a couple of streets away in Trafalgar Square.
Above The containers in which runner beans are grown are positioned in dormer window alcoves to protect them from the wind.
Above centre, above right, below right and **below centre** Other crops on this rooftop allotment include red raspberries, the black tomato 'Indigo Rose', yellow raspberry 'All Gold' and 'San Marzano' plum tomatoes.

'The raspberries in the Fruit Garden, which has a view of Charing Cross station, produce succulent fruit.'

The final garden is the Cottage Garden, a kaleidoscopic vista of colour and form. Sweet peas (*Lathyrus odoratus*), honeysuckle (*Lonicera*) and rudbeckia grow alongside pittosporum, cordyline and pyracantha. Like the other three gardens, the effect is charmingly pretty, but it also has a function – to encourage pollinators over a long season.

NO PROTECTION
The entire roof garden is organic. The plants are grown in ordinary compost, with the addition of calcified seaweed. There is a drip-feed irrigation system – goodness knows how many metres of tubing it uses – but there is no netting, or fleece, or any other protective measures, because it is too windy.

There are upsides and downsides to roof gardens. You do not get squirrels, but you do suffer from pigeons. You do not find slugs and snails, but the drying effects of sun and wind that keep molluscs at bay make for difficult conditions in which to

grow plants. This is extreme gardening, and every feature in this hostile terrain is utilized. The air-conditioning vents provide constant warmth for anything that is slightly tender.

Beefsteak tomato plants are grown almost like a pumpkin, with the main stalk spiralling round the container rather than being trained upright. Other tomato plants are truncated, so they do not put energy into producing trusses that will never ripen.

PHILANTHROPIC TRADITION

Coutts and Co. traces its history back to 1692, when it was founded – like so many of Britain's banking institutions – by Scots. It is now the wealth division of the Royal Bank of Scotland group. One of the most famous members of the Coutts family is Angela Burdett-Coutts (1814–1906), who inherited her grandfather Thomas Coutts's fortune of £1.8 million when he died in 1837. Being a great philanthropist, it was Lady Burdett-Coutts who had the statue of Greyfriars Bobby erected outside the Greyfriars Kirk in Edinburgh in memory of the little dog who refused to leave his master's grave.

The wooden containers in which the plants are grown in the Coutts Skyline Garden are a reminder of this philanthropic tradition. They were supplied especially for Coutts by The Clink Charity, which aims to reduce reoffending of ex-offenders by training them for jobs in the hospitality industry.

The boardroom at the Coutts London headquarters contains a superb Chinese mural. It is actually wallpaper, painted on mulberry paper, and mounted on wooden panels. It shows Chinese life as it was in the late eighteenth century, and it was given to Thomas Coutts by George Macartney, who led the first British embassy to China, in an attempt to negotiate a favourable trading agreement for Britain. It is a sort of documentary account of agriculture and domestic life, and in one section it depicts monkeys picking the leaves of oolong tea. According to tradition, the monks trained the monkeys to access the choice leaves from tea plants growing in the Wuyi Mountains. Oolong tea is then produced using a unique process, in which the leaves are dried in hot sunshine so that they wither and curl.

Coutts now imports its very own blend of this sought-after tea, and it is offered to guests after lunch in the private dining rooms. (Although still described as Monkey-Picked oolong, it is no longer picked by monkeys.) Those lucky enough to be offered tea usually opt for mint or lemon verbena, picked from the herbs outside and thrust into a pot of boiling water.

Above left Bright colours proliferate in the Cottage Garden.
Above Different lavender varieties and species grow in the Herb Garden.
Far left and left As well as looking pretty, the flowers of plants such as rudbeckia and lavender help to attract pollinators over a long season.

HIGH SOCIETY

KENSINGTON ROOF GARDENS, KENSINGTON

David Lewis, head gardener at the Kensington Roof Gardens, is in the enviable position of being able to look down on his garden from a cocktail bar while at the same time admiring a panoramic view of the London skyline. Not that he spends much time in the cocktail bar, of course – he is far too busy looking after his gardens. It is mainly the guests at Babylon, the Roof Gardens restaurant, as well as those attending the many parties, launches and awards ceremonies that take place in the gardens, who have the leisure to sit back and admire, drink in hand.

Kensington Roof Gardens is an astonishing 0.6-hectare/ 1½-acre plot 30 m/100 ft above street level. They were designed by landscape architect Ralph Hancock and constructed between 1936 and 1938 on the rooftop of what used to be the Derry & Toms department store in Kensington High Street.

Robin Hull is an expert on Hancock, who was born in Cardiff in 1893. He says that the architect came to the notice of Trevor Bowen, vice-president of Barkers, which owned Derry & Toms, after Hancock had designed the Gardens of the Nations at the Rockefeller Center in New York City; each garden had a national theme. Bowen visited New York on a fact-finding mission, and decided that he wanted the same approach for the Derry & Toms Roof Gardens. Hancock therefore followed the same pattern, with three themed gardens – Spanish, Tudor and Woodland – containing more than seventy trees, a stream stocked with fish and the famous resident flamingos.

During the three decades after the gardens opened in May 1938, said Hull, the one shilling (five pence) entrance fee raised more than £120,000 for local hospitals. Two visitors' books, now in Kensington library, contain the signatures of celebrities such as Sir John Gielgud, Leslie Howard, Sir Cedric Hardwicke and Ivor Novello as well as those of royalty, such as Queen Mary, King Haakon VII of Norway, Queen Maria of Yugoslavia and Prince Bernhard of the Netherlands.

In 1974, the entire Art Deco Derry & Toms building was taken over by Biba, the British fashion company that epitomized the late 1960s and early 1970s with its smoky colours and retro appeal. The Roof Gardens became the haunt of rock stars such as Mick Jagger, David Bowie and Marc Bolan. Sadly, Biba was forced to close in 1975, and for a while the gardens sank into obscurity.

PRACTICAL APPROACH

Today, at nearly eighty years old, the gardens have changed remarkably little. They have a maturity that makes it difficult

Photographs by Hugo Rittson Thomas

The high brick walls of Kensington Roof Gardens help to foster the illusion that you are still at ground level – until you look through the round windows.

to remember that you are six floors up from street level.
It is even more surprising when you realize that everything,
including the trees, is planted in only 45 cm/18 inches of soil.

Since 1981, the Kensington Roof Gardens have been
rented by Sir Richard Branson's Virgin group, while the
German-owned company Sirosa bought the freehold of the
building in 2013. The gardens are protected by preservation
orders, and a Grade II listing, but that does not deter Lewis
from having a very practical approach to gardening the space.
For such an ornamental garden, he has managed to squeeze
in an astonishing amount of fruit and veg, including figs,
almonds and pumpkins.

The bar terrace of the restaurant looks out over the
Woodland Garden, where a stream meanders through
native British trees. At the western end is the pool where the
flamingos live, and a *trompe-l'oeil* gate in the wall, which is
flanked by two plaques commemorating Hancock and Bowen.
The Hancock plaque was unveiled only in 2012, by members
of the Roof Gardens gardening club.

It has long been felt by Hancock's supporters, such as
Robin Hull, that Bowen took rather too much of the credit
for the Roof Gardens, but Lewis takes a more pragmatic view.
After all, he said, it was Bowen's idea. He relates how one
of the gardening club, which meets once a month on Sunday

mornings for bacon sandwiches and champagne, used to work
in the Roof Gardens during the 1940s and 1950s. This employee
needed a loan in order to buy a house, and his manager at Derry
& Toms personally guaranteed it.

FORMAL LAYOUT

The Woodland Garden leads round to the Tudor Garden,
complete with mock Tudor stonework and herringbone
brickwork, and typically English plants such as roses. Next to
it, the Spanish Garden is a kaleidoscope of colour, with poppies
(*Papaver*), verbascum and geums in early summer giving way
to dahlias in the central borders, and subtropicals such as
tetrapanax, yuccas and trachycarpus providing both structure
and a lush backdrop.

The campanile, or bell tower, at the northern end of the
Spanish Garden was hit by a bomb during the Second World
War, but has since been rebuilt. It echoes the towering spire of

'Three themed gardens - Spanish,
Tudor and Woodland - contain more
than seventy trees.'

Opposite The Spanish Garden, with its campanile and rows of cypresses, was the inspiration for a show garden at RHS Chelsea Flower Show in 2014.
Top Cheerful red walls here contribute to a Mediterranean feel.
Above Yuccas and trachycarpus provide an evergreen backdrop.
Right Dahlias and sunflowers take centre stage in high summer.

St Mary Abbots, on the corner of Kensington High Street and Kensington Church Street.

The layout is formal in the Spanish Garden, but the planting is not too straitjacketed, partly because it is more practical not to have everything in rigid groups and lines. 'If you plant your tulips in a grid pattern,' explains Lewis, 'and someone picks one, or it gets blown over, it is very noticeable. If they are in random groups, you do not see it so much.'

Do guests pick the flowers? 'We had a wedding once, where the children picked all the tulips while their parents were in the dining room. The bride was very upset,' he recalls.

Considering the footfall in the gardens, it is a wonder that Lewis and his team ever have an opportunity to get down to some serious maintenance without being overrun by people.

Every June, the gardens play host to the annual pre-Wimbledon tennis tournament party, attended by the world's top players. There is a nightclub every Friday and Saturday, and the rest of the time the venue is hosting weddings, corporate events, product launches and awards ceremonies. The restaurant is always busy, especially in summer.

It is a common misconception in London that the Kensington Roof Gardens are closed to the public. They are open, but only when there is not a function taking place, which is not very often.

If you book a table for lunch at Babylon, it is worth asking if you can have a look round afterwards.

AESTHETIC ENHANCEMENT

You sense that, for Lewis, his is more than just a nine-to-five gardening job. It was his idea to start the gardening club, and he feels strongly that the Roof Gardens should have a role in helping to promote horticulture in London.

Being a politics graduate from what is now City University in London, he subscribes to the philosophy of Tsunesaburo Makiguchi, who believed in what is called value-creation, the values being beauty, gain and good. 'Beauty' is generally defined as aesthetic enhancement; 'gain' as anything that enriches a person's life; and 'good' as the things that benefit society as a whole. It is a fairly safe bet that Mr Makiguchi would have regarded the Roof Gardens as fulfilling all these criteria.

When you mention the Kensington Roof Gardens to Londoners, the word 'flamingo' will soon crop up. The birds seem to take British winters in their long-legged stride, and seem equally unperturbed by awards ceremonies and product launch parties.

CHAPTER FIVE
PRIVATE PARADISES

A FAMILY AFFAIR

ST GEORGE'S ROAD, TWICKENHAM

For centuries, the quiet suburb of Twickenham has been used as a retreat from the bustle of London city life. It was here that the poet Alexander Pope used the profits from his translation of Homer to buy a villa beside the Thames in 1719, while Horace Walpole built his Gothic Revival fantasy, Strawberry Hill (see page 30), in the mid-eighteenth century. Other literary residents have included Charles Dickens, Alfred Lord Tennyson and Walter de la Mare, while the painter J.M.W. Turner both designed and built a country retreat for himself and his father.

Turner's house is currently undergoing restoration, a project with which Richard and Jenny Raworth will have sympathy. They bought their house, a few streets away from Sandycombe Lodge, in 1973, and have since transformed it into the sort of house and garden that would please the most demanding aesthete.

At the time, the Raworths had two small daughters – the elder, Sophie, is now one of the BBC's best-known newsreaders, while Kate is a sculptor – and friends advised them not to take on such a massive task. But the couple were shrewd enough to see the potential of the wrecked site.

Photographs by Marianne Majerus

Beneath a wall swathed in *Rosa* 'Constance Spry' thrive moisture-loving plants such as *Iris sibirica*, hostas, astrantia and ligularia.

At the rear, the Raworths' garden backs on to the St Margaret's Pleasure Grounds, a remnant of the Twickenham Park estate given by the Earl of Essex – a favourite of Queen Elizabeth I – to Sir Francis Bacon in 1595. For the Raworths, however, these communal gardens provided a borrowed landscape. It is difficult to believe that the centre of London is only 15 kilometres/9½ miles away.

London gardens have their limitations – most notably when it comes to light and size – but they also allow their owners a certain amount of freedom. Behind high walls you can create pretty much anything you like, without having to worry about whether it is historically appropriate or sits comfortably within the surrounding landscape.

GARDEN 'ROOMS'

The Raworths' garden is unusual in that it wraps around the house on three sides. They have split it into 'rooms', which both increase the sense of space and allow them to create a variety of atmospheres. It may seem contradictory that dividing the garden into smaller parts makes it seem bigger, but by doing so you lose the sense of an ultimate boundary that you get in a garden which reveals itself all at once.

At the front of the house, the Raworths have dispensed with a lawn. Instead, they lowered the level to create a sunken garden,

which they planted with grasses and libertia. It also features two traditional Cretan pots. Planted between the steps, in dense strips, are to be found small-leaved *Cotoneaster procumbens* 'Queen of Carpets'.

The path to the front door is guarded by a platoon of topiary, while a second path leading round the house is bordered by roses and clematis. The 'rooms' are created with yew (*Taxus*) hedges, and the first of these features a sculpture flanked by topiary spirals and two beds that contain potted bedding. Jenny feels this is a good way of providing seasonal interest as it is much easier to replant containers rather than dig everything up. A spring display of white tulips, for example, might make way for the snowy trumpets of white brugmansia in summer.

LAYERS OF GREEN AND WHITE

The path continues past the conservatory, where a collection of pelargoniums echoes the summer-pudding colours of the cushions, and brings you to the dining area and the lawn behind the house. The dining area, on the left, is shaded by a pergola, and separated from the lawn, with its traditional exuberant herbaceous borders, by a bed of irises and lavender (*Lavandula*).

To the right, at the end of the lawn, a sculpture looks down on a froth of *Geranium maderense* and hostas. This is flanked by *Hydrangea arborescens* 'Annabelle', one of the most popular

Opposite above and **below** The bog garden was originally a pond, but the arrival of grandchildren inspired the Raworths to come up with a more child-friendly alternative.

Top A bed of *Iris* 'Jane Phillips', with a column of yew at either end, frames a view of the herbaceous border, and a *Cornus controversa* 'Variegata'.

Above In the front garden, roses and clipped box pyramids surround a sunken area planted with ornamental grasses.

varieties thanks to its tolerance of cold and drought, and to its cool white flowers. On the other side, a specimen of wedding cake tree (*Cornus controversa* 'Variegata') guards its corner jealously with spreading layers of green and white. Cottage garden favourites such as lychnis and even white rosebay willowherb (*Chamaenerion angustifolium* 'Album', syn. *Epilobium angustifolium* var. *album*) feature in the herbaceous borders, along with dahlias, roses and campanula.

The Raworths used to have a pond but felt it was potentially dangerous once the grandchildren were on the scene. Now it is a bog garden, and a decking path leads through hostas and daylilies (*Hemerocallis*) to the back of the house, providing a jungle circuit for adventurous small people.

DETERRING FOXES

The final 'room' is the Knot Garden, where a sculpture of an embracing couple sits amid the neatly trimmed box (*Buxus*). The sculpture was made by Kate, and Jenny Raworth recalls that they decided to put down permeable membrane to keep weeds at bay, but this attracted the attention of a local fox, who dug holes in it. They then had to lay a sheet of galvanized mesh, or chicken wire, to stop the intruder. It may console London gardeners plagued by these urban scavengers that even the best-organized plots have to cope with Mr Fox.

Top and **above** Pelargoniums thrive in the conservatory, where their colours are picked up in the chintz cushions on the chair.
Opposite above 'Doors' in the *Thuja plicata* hedges invite the visitor to explore the Knot Garden beyond.
Opposite below The sculpture at the centre of the Knot Garden is by Kate Raworth, one of the owners' two daughters.

CONTEMPORARY CHIC

FAIRFIELD, DULWICH VILLAGE

The red-brick, Queen Anne-style house at No. 9 Dulwich Village is the sort of property that prompts one to buy a lottery ticket. It may have been built in the 1920s, but it is classically elegant, set in a London village that is only ten minutes from the city centre by train. Yet it still retains its sense of intimacy and rural charm.

Looking at the facade, with its multi-paned windows and imposing front door, you may think you can guess what lies in the garden behind. A box (*Buxus*) parterre, perhaps, planted with lavender (*Lavandula*) and catmint (*Nepeta*), and a pergola wreathed in David Austin roses. In fact, there is none of these.

The glass walls of the vast living room look out on to a contemporary garden with a swimming pool in the foreground. Beside the pool, designed by ACQ Architects who remodelled the house, a long raised bed is planted with *Calamagrostis* × *acutiflora* 'Karl Foerster'. Beyond the pool, behind two painted rendered walls in vivid pink, lies a vegetable garden composed of raised beds. As the gardening writer Anna Pavord put it, in her column for *The Independent*: 'It is spectacular, superbly

designed, uncompromisingly modern, quite the best thing of its kind that I have seen.'

The first thing that strikes you is the simplicity of the whole garden's design. It is very architectural, based on rectangular blocks that unite both the swimming pool and the raised vegetable beds, as well as, beyond these, the stepped, monolithic hedge of yew (*Taxus*). Opposite the yew, a large oak (*Quercus*) is underplanted with box balls on a neat diagonal grid.

Scarcely have you paused to admire this – not only as a design feature but also as a neat solution to the problem of dry shade beneath the tree – than the central path entices you up to a second terrace, with a fishpond flanked by two raised beds planted with grasses and perennials such as golden rod (*Solidago*), penstemons and veronicastrum.

HORNBEAM HEDGES

From the house, it is not obvious that the garden is L-shaped. You are just beginning to wonder how big it really is when you spot a shallow flight of steps leading to a large lawn on the left that stretches away to a wooden deck at the far end. Either side of the lawn are corridors formed of hornbeam (*Carpinus*) hedges, the inner ones lower than the outer ones.

An opening in the hedge on the right of the lawn reveals a wild woodland area, with a garden shed, a compost heap and an

Photographs by Hugo Rittson Thomas

The bright pink walls in this garden, designed by Christopher Bradley-Hole, are reminiscent of the work of Luis Barragán, the Mexican architect famous for his use of colour and light.

impressive bug 'hotel' built from wooden pallets and gardening leftovers, such as bricks, fir cones, bamboo canes, string bags for collecting leaves, and bits of piping. Walk back down towards the Fishpond Terrace and the woodland area becomes a more formal line of white birches (*Betula*).

On the other side of the lawn, there is another opening in the hornbeam hedges. Good grief, there's more! Between the hedges and next door's fence, a mini orchard has been planted, with espaliers against the fence and free-standing trees in rough grass, accessed by informal curving timber steps.

Someone very clever has obviously been at work here, and it comes as no surprise to discover that the designer is Christopher Bradley-Hole. The garden has his trademarks: the sense of serenity you get from a design that is perfectly proportioned; and his attention to detail – the green roofs on the two little sheds behind the swimming pool, for example – that stops you drifting off into a blissful, Zen-like state and makes you want to explore further.

'The garden has the sense of serenity you get from a design that is perfectly proportioned.'

Opposite above The use of one plant, *Calamagrostis* × *acutiflora* 'Karl Foerster', heightens the impression of serenity.
Opposite below Pink tulips pick up the wall colour.
Top A limestone window offers a view of the rest of the garden.
Above Airy perennials create another change of pace.
Right Box balls provide interest and texture beneath the giant oak.

Top Wide shallow steps lead up through the raised beds of the Kitchen Garden.
Above Bluebells flourish in the woodland area.
Left White and wine-dark tulips against limestone steps creates a sophisticated partnership.

It is a cunning idea to put the Kitchen Garden behind the swimming pool, and it has several benefits. First, you do not have to walk very far to harvest your tomatoes or asparagus, which is useful if it is raining. Second, a lawn here would be impossible to maintain because of the big oak. Third, the raised beds are on a generous scale – because they have to be in proportion with the rest of the garden – so they are capable of sustaining an asparagus bed, a strawberry patch, a row of runner beans, a dozen tomato plants, sweetcorn, marrows and courgettes.

One of the most impressive things about the garden in Dulwich Village is its sense of privacy. It is hardly overlooked at all, despite the fact that the houses in the street behind look down into it. The white birches screen their view and, on the other three sides, mature trees provide a borrowed landscape that looks more like a country village than a London suburb.

LONDON'S LAST TOLL GATE

Dulwich has been a village since Saxon times – the name is thought to mean 'the damp meadow where dill grows' – and since 1619 it has been a centre of education and art. The Dulwich schools – including what is now Dulwich College – were founded by Edward Alleyn, the favourite actor of Elizabeth I, who bought the manor of Dulwich for £5,000 and set up a charitable foundation to educate poor children.

Much of Dulwich – 607 hectares/1,500 acres, including some private roads and what is thought to be London's last toll gate – is still owned by the Dulwich estate, set up to provide funds for the schools. Alleyn's art collection formed the nucleus of what is now the Dulwich Picture Gallery, designed by the architect Sir John Soane and opened to the public in 1817.

Despite its long history, much of Dulwich is not as old as it looks or feels. Although there are many Georgian properties, Dulwich College, which is one of the most impressive buildings in south London, was designed in 1870 by Charles Barry Jnr, son of the architect who designed the Houses of Parliament. It is the alma mater of the writer Raymond Chandler, the explorer Sir Ernest Shackleton and, more recently, the actor Chiwetel Ejiofor, the star of the film *Twelve Years a Slave*.

The 400-year reign of the Dulwich estate has protected the village from the sort of cheap, piecemeal, high-rise development that has afflicted other south London boroughs, and the new is carefully blended with the old. A bit like Christopher Bradley-Hole's garden design.

Above The fragrance of the lavender planted around the small fishpond scents this terrace, which is screened from neighbours' windows by young Himalayan birches.

THE ENGLISH TRADITION

ORMELEY LODGE, HAM

The name Ormeley Lodge may not mean anything to you unless you are an inveterate reader of the gossip columns. It is the exquisite Georgian house where Diana, Princess of Wales used to visit her friend Lady Annabel Goldsmith. Diana would come for Sunday lunch at Ormeley, near Richmond in south-west London, bringing her sons, Princes William and Harry. Lady Annabel was an old friend and confidante – a mother figure to the lonely princess who had become very wary of discussing her private life for fear that any disclosures would find their way on to the front pages of the tabloid press the following day.

DOG MEMORIALS

As the setting for Lady Annabel's annual garden parties, Ormeley Lodge may sound like a showpiece designed solely to impress, but in reality it is a very tranquil family garden, full of memories and children's toys.

It lies just inside Richmond Park, close to Ham Common and the village of Petersham, which together make this one of the prettiest areas of London. Ham Common, which runs

Photographs by Hugo Rittson Thomas

Paths are mown through the grass in the Orchard, where spring flowers include camassias, daffodils and cowslips.

past the front of the house, is a conservation area and the triangular section opposite Ham Gate looks like the archetypal village green. There is a pond with ducks, which creates a rural ambience for the residents of the elegant, eighteenth-century houses in warm red brick.

Ormeley Lodge, which was built in 1715, is Grade II* listed, and the front of the house, with its ornamental gates – praised by Nikolaus Pevsner as 'outstandingly fine' – is visible from Ham Gate Avenue. Lady Annabel has lived there since the 1970s, and Zac, Jemima and Ben – her three children by her second husband, Sir James Goldsmith – grew up there. (Zac Goldsmith is now Conservative MP for the local constituency, Richmond Park.)

The garden in front of the house, designed by Mary Keen, has large box (*Buxus*) 'plinths', from which containers planted with white pelargoniums emerge like ballerinas on *pointe*. A huge *Magnolia grandiflora* obviously enjoys the warmth of the brickwork on the right-hand side of the front door, while wisteria is trained across the full width of the house. It all looks very simple, and very cool.

A gate leads to a Knot Garden, designed by Arabella Lennox-Boyd, in two colours of box, with standard holly trees (*Ilex*) in the middle of each section. Beyond the Knot Garden, there are swings and a trampoline, and memorials to much-loved dogs,

some of which are antique and came from Wynyard Park, the family estate in County Durham where Lady Annabel spent much of her childhood.

Some of the older dog headstones are quite elaborate, with carved stone hounds, but the newer ones are distinguished by their charming epitaphs. One reads: 'Boris, June 1994–March 2009. Much-loved son of Barney and Bee. Ingenious thief in the kitchen. Missed by all.' Another pays tribute to 'Scruff, 2002–2012. The Perfect Dog'.

WILDFLOWER MEADOW

Behind the house, a formal terrace echoes the planting at the front, with more box 'plinths' around containers planted with white-flowering summer bedding. The white-painted furniture, with its unusual trellis design, is eighteenth century. It is carefully stored away every winter, and repainted once a year.

To the right of the terrace, an area known as the Paddock begins with an avenue of *Prunus* × *subhirtella* 'Autumnalis', again designed by Mary Keen, while a statue of a giant gorilla – a present from zoo-keeper John Aspinall to Sir James Goldsmith – lurks beneath a huge Atlas cedar (*Cedrus atlantica*). The grass in the Paddock is allowed to grow long, with paths mown through it. It is also home to some Buff Orpington chickens and a gypsy caravan.

From the Paddock you enter the Wild Garden, or Orchard, where spring bulbs, such as camassias and daffodils (*Narcissus*), grow amid a carpet of cowslips (*Primula veris*) in spring. This Orchard meadow, criss-crossed by more mown paths, features something that anyone who has aspirations to a wildflower meadow might like to copy, suggests head gardener Steven Hannigan. Around the edge of each meadow section is a strip, or border, where the earth is almost bare, and this is planted up in summer with annuals. Trying to get the balance right between flowers and grass in meadow planting is always tricky, and trying to seed into grass is near-impossible.

Hannigan's solution allows a froth of flowers around the outside while the middle bit is left to its own dishevelled devices. It also means that you can cut the meadow grass in mid- to late summer, and still have some floral action going on.

Above There is a clever balance of the formal and the spontaneous at Ormeley Lodge, where clipped yew hedges and neatly trimmed lawns contrast with exuberant planting.

Top Herbaceous planting around the lawn includes peonies and poppies.
Above The Knot Garden was designed by Arabella Lennox-Boyd.
Right A bench forms a focal point at the end of a yew allée.

Top A dog memorial is positioned at the centre of the Orchard.
Above The carved stone dogs were brought to Ormeley Lodge by
Lady Annabel from her childhood home, Wynyard Park.
Left *Narcissus poeticus* var. *recurvus* blooms in the Paddock.
Opposite The gates at the rear of Ormeley Lodge open on to
Richmond Golf Club, but the effect is of parkland stretching beyond.

AVIARIES AND APPLE TREES

To the right of the Orchard, behind a high yew (*Taxus*) hedge, is the Kitchen Garden, with its neat rows of vegetables, and what looks like a fruit cage until you get a bit closer and realize that it is an aviary, with chirping budgerigars and cockatiels.

At the back of the garden, high ornamental gates look out on to Richmond Golf Club. It comes as quite a shock to look up and see a group of golfers, but not as much of a shock as it is to get a golf ball through the greenhouse roof, says Hannigan drily. He has prudently replaced the glass with polycarbonate.

Walking back towards the house, past the massive rhino grazing beneath the apple (*Malus*) trees (another present to Sir James Goldsmith), you reach the swimming pool, which is surrounded by magnolia, clematis and ornamental vines (*Vitis*). Behind a hedge near the pool is another aviary, which is home to a collection of canaries. From here, the path leads down beside the tennis court to a little arbour, clothed in scented *Trachelospermum jasminoides*, from where the less energetic members of the Goldsmith family can watch the play. Hannigan designed the beds either side of this garden walk. They are planted with herbaceous perennials between piers of bay (*Laurus nobilis*), and feature a large tree of heaven (*Ailanthus altissima*).

Other notable trees at Ormeley Lodge are the tulip tree (*Liriodendron tulipifera*) behind the house, and those at the

'The older dog headstones are quite elaborate, with carved stone hounds, but the newer ones have charming epitaphs.'

end of the main lawn, which include two *Liquidambar styraciflua* and a *Catalpa bignonioides*.

A low box hedge separates the terrace from the main lawn, which is surrounded by wide borders planted with shrubs and ebullient herbaceous perennials such as *Helianthus* 'Lemon Queen'.

Although box blight is not a problem here, Lady Annabel always has dogs. How does the box hedging stand up to their 'attentions'? 'We get the odd yellow bit,' says Hannigan, 'but nothing very serious. Although I have been known to touch up the corners of the hedge with a bit of green paint just before a party.' Now that is not the sort of thing you ever read in the gossip columns.

A CITY SANCTUARY

LANSDOWNE ROAD, HOLLAND PARK

The phrase *rus in urbe* is somewhat overused, but it really does sum up the garden belonging to Lady Amabel Lindsay in Holland Park. At Lansdowne Road it looks as if an English country garden has been picked up and magically transported to the heart of west London.

The centrepiece is a 200-year-old mulberry tree (*Morus nigra*), which extends a protective canopy over a Coalbrookdale cast-iron bench. From here the view is of soft, misty colours in the borders, where foxgloves (*Digitalis*), tulips (*Tulipa*), peonies (*Paeonia*), roses and iris in late spring give way to asters, penstemons, echinacea, *Gaura lindheimeri* and Japanese anemones (*Anemone* × *hybrida*) in late summer. Hollyhocks (*Alcea*), *Verbena bonariensis* and a lavatera add height, as do the dark red obelisks that support late-flowering clematis.

When in flower, pots of *Lilium regale* are dotted around the garden, to provide scent, and Lady Amabel also grows Chinese tree peonies (*Paeonia suffruticosa*) in pots, so that they too can be displayed when at their most spectacular. This is a real London garden trick: where space is tight, growing plants in containers

allows you to bring them into the spotlight when they are in flower and remove them from view when they are past their best.

A brick pergola provides the framework for wisteria, clematis and a variegated trachelospermum. It is also a useful shady place to put the lily and peony pots when they are not in flower.

At the end of the pergola is the entrance to the greenhouse, which is a lean-to design that would be more like a conservatory were it not for the fact that it is not attached to the house. It contains a display of climbing pelargoniums in shades ranging from white through to deep red. A golden robinia rises above it, helping to block out the view of the neighbouring houses.

MULBERRY TREE

Lady Amabel has lived in Lansdowne Road for fifty-five years, and during that time the layout of the garden has hardly changed. Behind the main lawn, with its mulberry tree, a path leads round to the back of the garden to a shady area dominated by a huge bay tree (*Laurus nobilis*) and planted mainly with shrubs such as callicarpa and azalea (*Rhododendron*).

Two swans, each rising from a coronet, sit either side of the steps leading down from the drawing room to the garden and these represent the Lindsay family crest. It is all very romantic and very English – until you start looking closely and spot the Chinese-style bird table, and the Indian stone carvings, and the

Photographs by Hugo Rittson Thomas

Lady Amabel Lindsay's garden is the archetypal Englishwoman's plot, with pinks and blues predominating in the colour scheme.

Top The dark red of a Chinese-style bird table is picked up by the obelisks that support clematis in the border opposite.
Above The relief on the wall of the terrace shows Marcus Aurelius and his wife Faustina and is a copy of one at Wilton House.

Salvia confertiflora in a pot on the terrace. The stone relief showing the Roman emperor Marcus Aurelius and his wife Faustina is, however, not Italian but a copy of one at Wilton House, in Wiltshire.

Further inspection of the terrace reveals quite a few exotic specimens, such as datura and abutilon, amid a collection of salvias, fuchsias (including *F. microphylla* subsp. *hemsleyana* with its tiny, magenta flowers) and pelargoniums.

ANCESTRAL PRECEDENT

Lady Amabel, like many English gardeners, does not assault your ears with a list of botanical Latin names. She is extremely self-deprecating, and were it not for the fact that the English garden look is much more difficult to achieve than its artless effect suggests, you might be fooled into thinking that she had hardly anything to do with the garden at all. However, you can tell from the way that she talks about her plants that she knows every centimetre of this garden, and is firmly in control.

There is a good ancestral precedent for this: she is one of the descendants of John Lindley (whose father was an illegitimate son of Lord Halifax). Her aunt is Lindley's great-great-granddaughter. Lindley, a botanist who trained with Sir Joseph Banks, went on to become professor of botany at

Top In early spring, camellias take centre stage at Lansdowne Road.
Above Spring bulbs attractively carpet the ground.
Left The bronze sculpture is one of many artworks in the house and garden. Lady Amabel's late husband, Patrick, was a former chairman of the auctioneers Christie's.

Top Access to the back of the deep main border, seen here planted with tulips in spring, is provided by a hidden path from the pergola to the conservatory.

Above Climbing pelargoniums enjoy the protection of the lean-to conservatory.

Left Lady Amabel loves cottage-garden favourites such as perennial cornflowers, peonies, hardy geraniums, hollyhocks and roses.

Opposite *Erysimum* 'Bowles's Mauve' makes a spectacular display in spring and, if deadheaded, will flower all year.

'It is as if an English country garden has been magically transported to the heart of west London.'

London University, and it was on his recommendation that Kew Gardens was given to the nation. The Royal Horticultural Society library in Vincent Square is named after him. 'A cousin of mine has a Lindley collection at his garden in Pewsey, and there is a Lindley corner at the Chelsea Physic Garden. I suppose I ought to have one too,' remarks Lady Amabel.

Not in the front garden, one hopes, because this is a wonderful melange of lavenders (*Lavandula*) in blues and pinks. *Erysimum* 'Bowles's Mauve' tumbles down a low wall beneath *Rosa* Pearl Drift, which is a hybrid of *R.* 'Mermaid' and *R.* 'New Dawn'. In spring, the front garden is thickly carpeted with bluebells (*Hyacinthoides*) and camassia either side of the wide, flagged path that leads to the front door. It is difficult to believe that Holland Park tube station is only a short walk away.

Not that Holland Park is an aggressively urban neighbourhood. Like many areas of London, it was rural until the beginning of the nineteenth century, when plans for a new housing development on land belonging to the Ladbroke family were prepared by the architect Thomas Allason. Most of Lansdowne Road was built in the 1840s, and it was named after the Lansdowne area of Cheltenham, where the developers, Pearson Thompson and Richard Roy, had been based.

BOHEMIAN INFLUENCE

The layout of the Ladbroke estate echoes Thompson and Roy's Montpellier estate at Cheltenham, and the use of the names 'Lansdowne' and 'Montpelier' for streets within the development suggest that this was deliberate, even if Montpellier/Montpelier are spelt differently.

The population of Holland Park, like its neighbours Notting Hill and Ladbroke Grove, has always been an intriguing mix. The Holland Park Circle, a group of artists including Frederic Leighton, George Frederick Watts and the sculptor Sir Hamo Thornycroft were based in Melbury Road and Holland Park Road – 12 Holland Park Road is now the Leighton House Museum.

Lansdowne House, at 1 Lansdowne Road, was built to provide flats for struggling artists. It later became a recording studio, catering for musicians ranging from Lonnie Donnegan to John Lennon. Thank goodness that some tranquil places still remain, and Lady Amabel's garden is definitely one of them.

ART MEETS PLANT LIFE

THE BISHOPS AVENUE, HAMPSTEAD

Even if you did not know that The Bishops Avenue was one of the world's wealthiest residential districts, it would start to dawn on you as you strolled down the road. In most London streets, it takes a matter of seconds to walk from No. 1 to No. 19. In The Bishops Avenue, it takes a good ten minutes.

Most of the housing plots here measure 0.8–1.25 hectares/ 2–3 acres. The properties themselves exhibit a variety of architectural styles – Tudorbethan timbers and Arts and Crafts leaded windows; Dutch gables and neo-Georgian porticos; red brick, white render, green slates and any number of hipped roofs.

The bishop from whom the road takes its name was Wealdhere, or Waldhere, Bishop of London from 693 to some time between 705 and 716. He was granted the land in 704, possibly by Aethelred of Mercia, and it remained church property until 1894, when the Church of England began to let building plots. By the early twentieth century, the church had decided to sell the plots rather than lease them.

One of the most expensive properties in the road, Toprak Mansion, was sold in 2008 for £50 million to Nursultan

Photographs by Hugo Rittson Thomas

Trachycarpus fortunei and phormiums create an exotic ambience – redolent of the Riviera – beside the tennis court.

Nazarbayev, the president of Kazakhstan, and ten of the sixty-six houses in The Bishops Avenue are owned by the House of Saud, the Saudi royal family.

Sadly, many of the houses – including three Saudi-owned mansions – are derelict. Ceilings have fallen in, their front gates are boarded up and damp has started to attack the interiors.

LONDON CLAY

From a gardening point of view, conditions are surprisingly damp here, given that the neighbourhood is on comparatively high ground: it is 91 m/300 ft above sea level. Two streams – Dollis Brook and Mutton Brook – pass through this area on their way to Hendon, where they merge to form the river Brent. Mutton Brook flows underground from its source in Cherry Tree Wood, East Finchley, and comes to the surface just after The Bishops Avenue, before flowing through the nearby parks.

The soil is mainly London clay, which is notoriously hard to work. It is slow to warm in spring, and quick to compact in dry periods, which means that trying to maintain a lawn is something of a challenge.

Bob Hughes, who is in charge of maintaining the garden featured on these pages, knows this only too well. The size and design of the house means that the garden to the rear is very secluded, and so difficult growing conditions for grass. The house

'You find yourself scrutinizing every
wheelbarrow and spade to check that
it is not a priceless installation.'

is modern, built in 1998 and designed by Stephen Marshall
Architects. It looks a bit like a giant fortified wall or Aztec
temple, with enormous glass doors that can open up to create the
effect of a courtyard on the ground floor.

The large terrace, which has several seating areas, curves
round to link up with the recreation wing with its swimming
pool that has both inside and outside sections. The terrace is
planted very simply, with colourful bands of bedding – pansies
in winter, and New Guinea impatiens in summer – amid
structural evergreen topiary.

A large lawn, about 0.4 hectares/1 acre in size, balances the
monolithic lines of the house. It is pristine, mown with stripes,
and then cross-mown to give a chequerboard effect. To keep this
lawn looking good, Hughes uses a pedestrian petrol mower, a
Hayter 56, which is about the largest you can get before moving
up to a ride-on model, and he obtains good results, considering
that he has a constant battle with moss.

At either end of this lawn are two Modified Social
Benches, by the Danish artist Jeppe Hein, and these are
the first clue that all is not what it seems to be in this
garden. Hein's benches typically have some sort of subtle
distortion – the middle slat of the bench might form a
spiral, for example, or suddenly change direction. They
catch you out – they look normal at first glance, but
even if you do not notice the distortion it registers at a
subconscious level, and you find yourself taking a second
look to see why your brain is not totally happy with the
first impression.

While you are looking at the Hein benches and
wondering what it is about them that is not quite right,
you might catch a glimpse of the garden shed on the
terrace to the right of the swimming pool. Apart from the
turquoise-blue fake palm tree beside it, it initially looks
like a bog-standard garden shed – the sort of 1.75-m ×
1.2-m/6-ft × 4-ft one you buy at any DIY store or garden
centre. In fact, it is an artwork by the Brazilian artist
Alexandre da Cunha.

In front of the south-facing wall of the recreation
wing, with its face lifted to the sun, is an Antony Gormley
sculpture in cast iron. Like many of his works, the figure
is cast from the artist's body, but this one is encased in

Opposite The large expanse of lawn is in marked contrast to the woodland areas of the garden, where shrubs such as *Pittosporum tobira* and *Fatsia japonica* provide evergreen interest.
Top Behind the pink cosmos is a 'Modified Social Bench' by Jeppe Hein.
Above The outdoor gym is like an adventure playground for adults, with equipment designed for weight-training.
Right The Jeppe Hein bench is positioned in the shade of a huge oak tree. The coiled slat can be used as a headrest.

Top The Japanese Garden is here seen through the glass walls
of the summer house.

Above Carefully placed rocks, a stone lantern and an azalea are
traditional elements in a Japanese Garden, as is the moss.

Left There is no ground-cover planting or grass in the Japanese
Garden – just skilfully raked gravel and moss.

Opposite The summer house is framed by mature trees and shrubs,
which hide the boundaries of the garden and give the impression of
thick woodland that goes on far beyond. Nearby Hampstead Heath
is an important refuge for wildlife.

a shroud or chrysalis, which gives it an extra intensity. Another Gormley work, one of his Quantum Cloud series, stands just inside the house. By now, you are beginning to realize that this garden belongs to someone who collects and loves art – and so you find yourself scrutinizing every wheelbarrow or spade to double-check that it is in fact a tool and not some priceless installation.

The children's climbing frame, for example: is it a playground or a piece of art? It turns out to be a playground, although the series of wheels and pulleys and what look like see-saws is an outdoor gym designed for adults. Meanwhile, the tennis court, with its screen of phormiums, trachycarpus and eucalyptus, is simply a tennis court.

Gardens, or parks, make good spaces for such sculpture. The ever-changing light, and the varied background of textures and shapes that the planting provides, enhance the impact of the artwork. Using your garden as a gallery plays havoc with a lawn, however. Most collectors want to change pieces around on a fairly regular basis, and news of the arrival of a new sculpture and its attendant forklift trucks or cranes is met with mixed feelings by Hughes. However, he admits that he had little knowledge of art before he came to this garden seven years ago, and he has enjoyed learning to appreciate his employers' collection.

JAPANESE GARDEN

Most of the garden is surrounded by mature trees. An impressive oak (*Quercus*) dominates the view to the south-east, while the southern boundary features a woodland area with pines (*Pinus*), acers and contorted hazel (*Corylus avellana* 'Contorta').

Next to this woodland area is the Japanese Garden – Hughes's favourite part. It is composed of rocks amid raked gravel, and a selection of acers behind a hand-tied bamboo fence. In early summer, azaleas (*Rhododendron*) bloom in vibrant pinks and reds.

A little summer house, a simple, modern design in wood and glass, looks on to the Japanese Garden. An acer is planted in the centre of the summer house, in what is effectively a glass box that is open to the sky. On the other side, where the woodland walk begins, there are more acers, and the combined effect of the glass and the repetition of the acers is a blurring of the boundaries so that you cannot see where the trees end and the building begins.

Although Hughes may wage war on moss in the main lawn, his battle in the Japanese Garden is to keep grass from growing up through the carpet of moss. The irony is not lost on him, and in this garden full of art he would probably be comforted by the great eighteenth-century landscape architect William Kent's view that 'all gardening is landscape painting.'

STAR OF NOTTING HILL

LADBROKE SQUARE GARDEN, NOTTING HILL

Ladbroke Square Garden is a good example of one of those extraordinary London juxtapositions, whereby turning a corner or diverting down a side road can take you from the bustle of the big city to the relative peace of a residential retreat in a few paces.

At almost 2.8 hectares/7 acres, Ladbroke Square Garden is thought to be the largest garden square in London. Yet the thousands of tourists who throng the Portobello Road market, only one street away, will probably never notice it or even walk past it. This is probably just as well, for the residents who use the Garden value their privacy.

It is a common misconception that if you live in a garden square, you are automatically entitled to a key. In most cases, there is a 'catchment area' for keyholders, who have to pay an annual fee. For Ladbroke Square Garden you have to live within 100 yards of the railings in order to be eligible for membership, which costs £240 a year.

Security is tight at most London garden squares, vulnerable as they are to vandalism and theft. It is a particular concern at

Photographs by Hugo Rittson Thomas

The sphere sculpture in the old Victorian fountain area was installed in commemoration of the 150th anniversary of Ladbroke Square Garden.

Ladbroke Square Garden, because, unusually for the Ladbroke Estate, on one side the houses back directly on to the Garden. This has two benefits, however. First, you do not have to cross the road to get to the Garden. Second, although the houses have their own small gardens, they also share a borrowed landscape of trees and grass.

And what trees they are! The most impressive is a huge cut-leaved Turkey oak (*Quercus cerris*), whose branches – some supported on crutches – seem to writhe in every direction at improbable girth and length. Nearby is a cork oak (*Q. suber*) and a semi-evergreen Lucombe oak (*Q.* × *hispanica* 'Lucombeana'), which is a hybrid of Turkey oak and cork oak.

There are London planes (*Platanus* × *hispanica*), yews (*Taxus*), hollies (*Ilex*) of all descriptions, a collection of hawthorns (*Crataegus*) that includes the unusual *C. heterophylla*, with variable leaf shapes, and Chinese hawthorn (*C. pinnatifida* var. *major*), with its dark red berries as big as crab apples.

Talking of crab apples, these too are well represented in Ladbroke Square Garden. The *Malus* × *zumi* 'Golden Hornet' on the East Lawn and the *M.* × *zumi* 'Professor Sprenger' near the Victorian shelter which commemorates the writer and musician Miles Kington, who died of cancer at the age of sixty-six in 2008. Kington, a former columnist with *The Times* and *The Independent*, and one of the comedy trio Instant Sunshine,

worked part-time in the Garden in 1963, in the days, as he put it: 'before Hugh Grant was born, and people in Notting Hill could still remember the war, and the barrage balloons moored in Ladbroke Square'.

Here, Kington was referring to the Second World War, which deprived the garden of its metal railings; these were restored in 1962. The First World War also had an impact when, in 1916, bulb imports from the Netherlands ceased. It was decided that any existing bulbs should be left in the ground, and apparently the display the following year was better than in any previous year.

LARGE LAWNS

The Garden was originally part of the Kensington Hippodrome, an ambitious scheme built in 1837 by an entrepreneur called John Whyte. Its 56-hectare/140-acre site originally extended north-west from Notting Hill almost to Wormwood Scrubs, and was intended to rival Ascot and Epsom. However, it was not a financial success and so closed in 1842.

The land on which the Kensington Hippodrome stood was immediately scheduled for development, but hardly had work started on Kensington Park Road and Ladbroke Square when the developers also went bust. However, by 1853, building leases had been granted on the south side of Kensington Park Gardens,

which backs on to Ladbroke Square Garden, and Nos 10–22 were constructed to a design by the architect Thomas Allom, a founding member of what was to become the Royal Institute of British Architects.

Today, the layout of the Garden is remarkably similar to that shown in the first survey in 1863. Three large lawns, linked by paths, and lined with mature trees, offer both sunny open spaces and dappled shade. Along the southern pathway, the trees screen two playgrounds: one for small children; the other for their older brothers and sisters. There is also a den, with tree-stump seats, in what used to be a gardeners' compound.

Adults have a playground too, in the form of a tennis court, installed at the instigation of Dame Jennifer Jenkins, wife of the politician Roy Jenkins. In the 1960s, it was not uncommon to see Jenkins and his Labour colleague Tony Crosland playing doubles with their wives.

'The borders are packed with interest, from spring bulbs early in the year to asters in autumn.'

Opposite The houses in Kensington Park Gardens have direct access
to Ladbroke Square Garden via their back gardens.
Top A typical spring scene includes bluebells in flower beneath laburnum.
Above Rhododendrons make their colourful contribution in late spring.
Right The massive branches of the Turkey oak are supported by
'crutches'. It looks like something from a Salvador Dali painting.

Top The horse chestnut looks particularly magnificent when in full bloom.
Above The rose pergola, which has oak obelisks linked by rope swags, was inspired by a similar feature in the gardens of Aranjuez, near Madrid.
Left Hawthorn flowers bend towards the carpet of hardy geraniums.

Beside the tennis court, on the East Lawn, a huge *Eucalyptus gunnii* dominates a border planted with phormiums and *Beschorneria yuccoides*, whose glaucous leaves echo the foliage of the eucalyptus. The head gardener at Ladbroke Square Garden, Colin Derome, has made a pathway into the border beneath the tree, and its rust-coloured trunk glows in sunlight.

The lawn itself is bordered at the eastern edge by a pergola of rambling roses, trained on wooden obelisks that are linked by thick rope. One of the roses is 'Phyllis Bide', a creamy pink rambler that repeat-flowers, and the design was inspired by a similar feature in metal in the gardens of Aranjuez, near Madrid.

SPRING BULBS

Ladbroke Square Garden is one of the floweriest of all the London squares. Apart from the flowering shrubs and trees, the borders are packed with interest from early in the year, when the spring bulbs appear, to early autumn, when asters, *Geranium* Rozanne and caryopteris provide pools of vivid blue and violet. This is a deliberate move by horticultural adviser

Sarah Debenham, who wants not only to provide year-round interest but also to create the feel of a real garden.

Some London squares can look quite dark and feel almost claustrophobic, especially if they are not very big, because the trees and shrubs that screen the gardens from public view also block out the sun. At Ladbroke Square Garden, the sheer size of the site means this is not so much of a problem, but the residents like to maintain an evergreen screen, especially at the Ladbroke Grove end. As well as providing privacy, it also blocks out the noise of traffic.

There is an extraordinary sense of intimacy for a garden of this size. At the east end of the Broad Walk, there is a small gardener's cottage – marked on the original plan. The scale of this, as well as the urn (a copy of one at Osborne House) filled with summer bedding that marks the start of the walk, is welcoming rather than intimidating.

Beside the cottage, sheltered both by trees and the houses of Kensington Park Gardens, the planting is more conventional, with *Verbena bonariensis* and Japanese anemones (*Anemone* × *hybrida*). Further along the Broad Walk, subtropical specimens flourish, such as ginger lily (*Hedychium*), *Euphorbia mellifera*, *Arundo donax* var. *versicolor* and agaves. Whatever your horticultural tastes – trees, perennials, exotics – there is something here of interest. As long as you have a key, of course.

Above This is the entrance to the Broad Walk, where south-facing benches provide keyholders with a sunny spot in which to sit and read or relax. The urn is a copy of one at Osborne House, Queen Victoria's seaside palace on the Isle of Wight.

AN IMPRESSIVE PEDIGREE

CADOGAN ESTATE, KNIGHTSBRIDGE

If you have ever walked or taken the bus down Sloane Street, from Knightsbridge to Sloane Square, you will have passed Cadogan Place gardens – a vast green space with tennis courts, trees, shrubberies and lawns that provides an exclusive back garden for the residents of the surrounding houses.

London is famous for its garden squares (see Eccleston Square, page 114 and Ladbroke Square, page 190) and, although they are usually accessible only to residents, they add a verdant charm to the capital and provide a glimpse of greenery for passers-by.

The Cadogan Place gardens, however, have a particularly distinguished pedigree. They are the jewel in the crown of the Cadogan estate, owned for 300 years by the Cadogan family who, after the Duke of Westminster, are London's wealthiest landlords. The gardens were part of a development called Hans Town, built on land leased from Charles, 1st Earl Cadogan in 1777 by the architect Henry Holland. Charles's mother was the daughter of Sir Hans Sloane, benefactor of the Chelsea Physic Garden (see page 126), who had bought the Manor of Chelsea

in 1712. When Sloane died in 1753, he had no sons, and his estate was divided between his two daughters. The streets in Holland's new town were named in honour of the two families: Hans Crescent (behind Harrods), Sloane Street, Sloane Square, Cadogan Place and so on.

BUCOLIC CHARACTER

Chelsea in the early eighteenth century was still rural, but had been popular for centuries with the great and the good as a country retreat, thanks to the river – which made it possible to commute to Westminster and the City of London reasonably easily – and the fresh country air. Sir Thomas More's house, for example, on what is now Beaufort Street in Chelsea, inspired Henry VIII to acquire a manor house of his own, on what is now Cheyne Walk, near the junction with Albert Bridge.

The 'new towns' of the eighteenth century – Camden Town is one that still retains the word 'town' in its place name – were not an expansion of London itself. They were suburbs and were designed to be outside the capital, rather than part of it. The bucolic character of these places, many of which still had market gardens, fields and orchards, was part of the attraction. Then, as now, the affluent middle classes wanted homes that were shielded from the noise, chaos and dangers of city life, and Chelsea was an ideal choice.

Photographs by Hugo Rittson Thomas

Cadogan Square was once the site of a mansion owned by developer Henry Holland, son-in-law of Lancelot 'Capability' Brown.

By the time Henry Holland came to develop the Cadogan estate in the late eighteenth century, he had established a solid reputation among the nobility. He and his father had worked extensively with Lancelot 'Capability' Brown, and Holland was married to Brown's daughter, Bridget.

When Holland built himself a house in Hans Town, known variously as the Pavilion, or Sloane Place, it is said Brown laid out the 6.5 hectares/16 acres of grounds. No trace of this Palladian mansion remains, however, as the area was redeveloped 100 years later as Cadogan Square.

BOTANIC GARDEN
Cadogan Square garden is one of the twenty gardens that the Cadogan estate team maintains. Of these, the largest garden by far is Cadogan Place. It is actually two gardens, Cadogan Place South and Cadogan Place North, separated by Pont Street, home to one of London's historic green cabmen's shelters, and what appears to be an ever-present queue of traffic.

Until 1820 when the garden was redesigned as a public promenade, the southern garden was known as the London Botanic Garden. It had been laid out by William Salisbury, who had studied at the Chelsea Physic Garden. There were horticulture lectures and summer evening concerts, and glasshouses stood on the site of what is now the tennis courts.

Today, the oldest things in this part of the garden are probably the mulberry trees (*Morus*), said to have been planted by Charles II at the end of the seventeenth century, in an attempt to create a silk industry in England. If Charles II had planted all the mulberry trees that are attributed to him, he probably would not have had any time to dally with Nell Gwyn, but the trees in Cadogan Place are certainly very old. Their aged limbs seem to want to rest, like an elderly man leaning his elbows on a wall. At some point in the past twenty or thirty years, they have been fitted with metal braces, like calipers, and where they fit too tightly the branches have begun to grow around them.

Head gardener Ric Glenn believes it would be better to leave the trees to their own devices. He pointed to one section that had split away from the main trunk and was supported by its branches, which were resting on the ground. The whole section had regenerated, rooting itself into a caviaty in the trunk.

In the northern section of the Cadogan Place gardens, an impressive stand of mimosa (*Acacia dealbata*) also suffers from the results of modern 'improvements'. Glenn is from Australia, and when he first joined the Cadogan estate team eighteen months ago he could not understand why the mimosa – tough, drought-tolerant performers in their native south-east Australia – were the first trees in the gardens to suffer in dry spells. He then realized that because of the underground car park, built

Opposite The Cadogan estate gardens are funded by the keyholders, who pay an annual fee to use the gardens.

Top Spring blossom is a welcome reminder to Londoners that summer is on the way.

Above Foxgloves in the gardens are suggestive of the area's rural past.

Centre right Relaxed planting is less labour-intensive than caring for herbaceous borders.

Right An ancient mulberry tree lives on in Cadogan Place South.

Top The key to successful park design is to focus on variety – this little Knot Garden providing a contrast to the large lawns.
Above (clockwise from left) Irises, ornamental onions and cherry blossom.
Left *Trachycarpus fortunei* form evergreen pillars within the garden.
Opposite The long racemes of this white wisteria hang gracefully from a pergola in Hans Place.

in the 1970s, the trees were sitting in what was effectively a concrete bowl. The advent of the underground car park was also responsible for the demise of the Humphry Repton design for Cadogan Place North, which had been in place since 1806.

RELIABLE PERFORMERS

Maintenance of all the Cadogan estate gardens – whether they are the bigger ones such as Cadogan Square, or the smaller strips of planting, such as the row of plane trees (*Platanus*) on Pont Street, opposite Hans Place – is funded by the annual charges paid by keyholders. Each garden has its own budget. Those with lots of keyholders, such as Cadogan Square – surrounded by Victorian mansion flats built in the style christened 'Pont Street Dutch' by Sir Osbert Lancaster – have a larger income.

The garden in Hans Place, on the other hand, does not have many keyholders. Glenn is keen to create vistas through some of the shrubbery so that the people who live around Hans Place

– used by black cab drivers as a rat-run from Knightsbridge to Sloane Square – can see how attractive it is, and thus apply to use it. Its most noteworthy specimen is a massive *Parrotia persica*, thought to be one of the biggest in the UK.

The Chelsea microclimate allows subtropical plants such as tree ferns (*Dicksonia*) and loquats (*Eriobotrya japonica*) to grow unhindered by frost. Glenn has started to create a stumpery on the east side of Cadogan Place South, using *Dicksonia antarctica* as well as British native ferns, while his pride and joy is the garden's thriving *Wollemia nobilis*.

Rare plants will always make gardeners' hearts beat faster, but the bombproof stalwarts deserve just as much admiration. Two that deserve a particular mention at Cadogan Place gardens are *Liriope muscari* 'Big Blue', with its spikes of a really vivid violet, and *Geranium* 'Tanya Rendall', bred in Orkney by Richard Rendall and named after his daughter.

Liriope is a favourite with London gardeners because it provides slug-proof, drought-tolerant, evergreen ground cover beneath trees, but the geranium, which has small, magenta flowers above a mat of olive-green foliage, is not so widely known. It deserves to be: it looks wonderful sprawling beneath clumps of grasses. Perhaps its Sloane Street showcase, next door to some of the world's most expensive designer stores, will help bring it into fashion.

> 'Rare plants always make a gardener's heart beat faster, but the bombproof stalwarts also deserve our admiration.'

GREAT GARDENS OF LONDON MAP

Featured gardens

Other great gardens and parks

Enfield

Barnet

Harrow

Haringey

Redbridge

Waltham Forest

2   28

21

Brent   12

27   25

Islington   Hackney   Barking & Dagenham

Camden   5   23   9

7   16

Havering

Hillingdon   Ealing   30   23   City of London   19   24   Newham

26   2   Tower Hamlets

Kensington   Westminster   34   14   15   35   31   43

& Chelsea   8   44   17   9   30

13   18   17   6   1

Hammersmith   26   24   4   19   8   15

& Fulham   16   6   5   10   42   28   Southwark

45   32   46   7   22   36   4   1   Greenwich

41   29   40   3   20   Bexley   37

14   Lambeth

Hounslow

27   39   25   Wandsworth   Lewisham   11

20   21   10   12

29   22

Richmond   Bromley

upon Thames   3   33

13   Merton

Kingston   Sutton   Croydon

38   upon Thames

11

0   10 km

0   10 miles

VISITING INFORMATION
FOR FEATURED GARDENS

The following thirteen gardens do not open to the public: The Bishops Avenue, Cadogan Estate, Clarence House, Corsica Street, Coutts Skyline Garden, Fairfield, Henrietta Street, Ladbroke Square, Malplaquet House, The Old Vicarage, Petherton Road, Regina Road, Winfield House

At the time of publication, the other seventeen gardens open to the public at some time during the year. Many open for the Open Garden Squares weekend (www.opensquares.org) or National Gardens Scheme (www.ngs.org.uk). Always check opening times on the website before travelling.

① 10 Downing Street
London SW1A 2AA
Open to the public by ballot only, as part of the Open House Scheme. See website for full details, as security measures require photo ID etc.
www.events.openhouselondon.org.uk
building/4968

② The Bishops Avenue (not open to the public)

③ Bushy Park Allotments
Bushy Park, Hampton Hill TW12 2ST
Open to the public on the annual open day, usually held mid-July. Cleve West's plot is No. 6.
www.bushyparkallotments.org.uk

④ Cadogan Estate (not open to the public)

⑤ Chelsea Physic Garden
66 Royal Hospital Road, London SW3 4HS
Open to the public year-round
Tel: 020 7352 5646
www.chelseaphysicgarden.co.uk

⑥ Clarence House (not open to the public)

⑦ Corsica Street (not open to the public)

⑧ Coutts Skyline Garden (not open to the public)

⑨ Downings Roads Floating Gardens
31 Mill Street, London SE1 2AX
Open to the public for Open Garden Squares weekend, for National Gardens Scheme and by appointment
www.towerbridgemoorings.co.uk/floating-gardens

⑩ Eccleston Square
Pimlico, London SW1V 1PB
Open to the public under the National Gardens Scheme and the Open Garden Squares weekend
www.ecclestonsquaregardens.com

⑪ Eltham Palace
Court Yard, Eltham, London SE9 5QE
Open to the public from March to October and occasionally in winter
Tel: 0870 333 1181
www.elthampalace.org.uk

⑫ Fairfield (not open to the public)

⑬ Hampton Court Palace
East Molesey KT8 9AU
Open to the public every day except 24–26 December
Tel: 0844 482 7777
www.hrp.org.uk/hamptoncourtpalace

⑭ Henrietta Street (not open to the public)

⑮ Inner Temple
London EC4Y 7HL
Open to the public weekdays from 12.30 to 3 p.m.
Tel: 020 7797 8243
www.innertemple.org.uk/index/
the-inner-temple-garden

⑯ Kensington Roof Gardens
99 Kensington High Street, London W8 5SA
Open to the public by appointment
Tel: 020 7937 7994
www.roofgardens.virgin.com

⑰ Ladbroke Square (not open to the public)

⑱ Lansdowne Road
London W11 3LW
Open to the public once a year under National Gardens Scheme, usually in late May
www.ngs.org.uk

⑲ Malplaquet House (not open to the public)

⑳ Old English Garden
Battersea Park, London SW11 4NJ
Open to the public every day from 8 a.m. to dusk
Tel: 020 8871 7530
www.batterseapark.org/nature/gardens/
old-english-garden

㉑ The Old Vicarage (not open to the public)

㉒ Ormeley Lodge
Ham Gate Avenue, Richmond TW10 5HB
Open to the public once a year under the National Gardens Scheme
www.ngs.org.uk

㉓ Petherton Road (not open to the public)

㉔ Queen Elizabeth Olympic Park
Stratford, London E20 2ST
Open to the public at all times
Tel: 0800 072 2110
www.queenelizabetholympicpark.co.uk

㉕ Regina Road (not open to the public)

㉖ Royal College of Physicians
11 St Andrews Place, London NW1 4LE
Open to the public Monday to Friday from 9 a.m. to 5 p.m. excluding public holidays
Tel: 020 3075 1539
www.rcplondon.ac.uk/museum-and-garden

㉗ St George's Road
Twickenham TW1 1QS
Open to the public for National Gardens Scheme and by prior arrangement from May to July for groups of more than ten people
Tel: 020 8992 3713
www.raworthgarden.com

㉘ St Regis Close
Alexandra Park Road, London N10 2DE
Open to the public for National Gardens Scheme and by prior arrangement from April to October for groups of more than ten people
Tel: 020 8883 8540
Email: suebearlh@yahoo.com

㉙ Strawberry Hill
268 Waldegrave Road, Twickenham TW1 4ST
Open to the public every day from 10 a.m. to 6 p.m. except in December and January
Tel: 020 8744 1241
www.strawberryhillhouse.org.uk/gardens.php

㉚ Winfield House (not open to the public)

OTHER GREAT GARDENS
AND EVENTS

The gardens in this book represent some of the most fascinating backyards in London, but here now are some of the dozens more that are also worth visiting. Those that are run by the National Trust or English Heritage are usually accessible year-round, while gardens that open for charity under the National Gardens Scheme (NGS; www.ngs.org.uk) may be visited for only one afternoon a year. It is worth acquiring the NGS annual directory, known as *The Yellow Book*; a London section of this is also available separately.

In addition to garden shows and festivals, there are two major events in London every year that allow the public access to private spaces. These are the Open House weekend, which in 2014 included nearly eighty landscape projects, and the Open Squares weekend, which spans allotments and community gardens as well as London squares.

Many of the gardens and parks listed below are accessible year-round, but even these sometimes close for essential maintenance such as tree surgery, or because they are hosting events such as weddings or concerts. It is always best to check opening times in advance.

Gardens and parks

1 225a Brixton Road
London SW9 6LW
Open to public: One day a year, under the National Gardens Scheme
Architects Deborah Nagan and Michael Johnson created this two-level garden following the building of an extension, aiming to create a modern urban oasis using unusual materials, but with maximum floral impact. Nagan is active in the Chelsea Fringe, and has created gardens in London, Luxembourg and Canada.
Further information: deborah@naganjohnson. co.uk; www.ngs.org.uk

2 Barbican Centre Conservatory
Silk Street, London EC2Y 8DS
Open to public: Yes, see website for full details
The conservatory at the Barbican Centre was built at the request of residents to hide the huge fly towers, which store stage sets above the Barbican Theatre. It is the second-biggest conservatory in London, and now includes 2,000 tropical plants and trees, and aquariums containing exotic fish.
Further information: www.barbican.org.uk/ visitor-information/conservatory

3 Brompton Cemetery
Fulham Road, London SW10 9UG
Open to public: Yes, every day
Strange as it may seem today, Brompton Road Cemetery was designed to be a public garden as well as a graveyard. Its 16 hectares/39 acres are a haven for wildlife, despite the fact that it is still a working cemetery, managed by the Royal Parks. The neoclassical design and layout are by the architect Benjamin Baud.
Further information: www.royalparks.org.uk/ parks/brompton-cemetery

4 Buckingham Palace
London SW1A 1AA
Open to public: No
All right, you can't really visit the gardens of Buckingham Palace unless you are lucky enough to be invited to one of the queen's garden parties. But if you are travelling on the top of a Boris bus – one of the new Routemasters commissioned by Mayor of London Boris Johnson – you can catch glimpses. Take the No. 9 or No. 10 from Victoria to Hyde Park Corner.
Further information:
www.tfl.gov.uk/maps_/bus-route-maps

5 Camley Street Natural Park
12 Camley Street, London N1C 4PW
Open to public: All year, but best to visit between April and August
The Camley Street nature reserve is behind King's Cross St Pancras stations, and was created on the site of an old coal yard, beside the Regent's Canal. It provides a habitat for birds, butterflies and amphibians, and among the more unusual species spotted there are reed warblers, kingfishers and various bats.
Further information: www.wildlifetrusts.org/ reserves/camley-street-natural-park

6 Carlyle's House
24 Cheyne Row, London SW3 5HL
Open to public: Yes, see website for full details
Thomas Carlyle loved his garden, partly because he could smoke there: 'I can wander about in dressing gown and straw hat in it, as of old, and take my pipe in peace.' He also grew vegetables, in between receiving some of the world's greatest literary figures, who visited him here.
Further information:
www.nationaltrust.org.uk/carlyles-house

7 Chiswick House and Gardens
Burlington Lane, London W4 2RP
Open to public: Gardens open all year
A £12 million conservation project has restored these gardens to their eighteenth-century glory. The conservatory houses what is thought to be one of the oldest collections of camellias under glass, while the garden designed by William Kent is the birthplace of the English Landscape Movement.
Further information: www.chgt.org.uk

8 Clifton Nurseries Ltd
5A Clifton Villas, London W9 2PH
Open to public: All year (but check Christmas and Easter opening times)
Set in the picturesque area known as Little Venice, Clifton Nurseries may be London's oldest garden centre, but it is also one of the most up-to-date. Under the leadership of managing director Matthew Wilson, they have done show gardens for the Chelsea Fringe and RHS Chelsea Flower Show.
Further information: www.clifton.co.uk

9 Columbia Road Flower Market
Columbia Road, London E2 7RG
Open to public: Every Sunday, 8 a.m. until *c.*3 p.m.
This East End market sells everything from bedding plants to palms and banana trees. Many of the stallholders have been trading for thirty or forty years, and around them a range of eclectic shops has sprung up, offering interiors, garden and vintage items. It is the real London deal.
Further information: www.columbiaroad.info

10 Crystal Palace Park
Thicket Road, London SE19 2GA
Open to public: All year
The Crystal Palace which gives the park its name burned down in 1936. However, the model dinosaurs – Victorian England's version of Jurassic Park – are still delighting children almost 160 years after the park was opened, in 1856, by Queen Victoria. It now houses the National Sports Centre and one of the UK's largest mazes.
Further information: www.bromley.gov.uk/parks

11 **Down House**
Luxted Road, Downe BR6 7JT
Open to public: Yes, but times vary, see website for full details
The gardens at Down House inspired the work of Charles Darwin. You can still see the greenhouses where he studied the reproductive behaviour of plants, as well as the study where he wrote *On the Origin of Species*. Twelve of his experiments have been recreated in the grounds.
Further information:
www.english-heritage.org.uk/daysout/properties/home-of-charles-darwin-down-house

12 **Fenton House**
Hampstead Grove, London NW3 6SP
Open to public: Yes, but times vary, see website for full details
The gardens at this former seventeenth-century merchant's house, now owned by the National Trust, have remained almost unchanged for 300 years. Visitors can explore the formal gardens, vegetable gardens and orchards, where thirty varieties of apples are grown. The balcony of the house offers a superb view of London.
Further information:
www.nationaltrust.org.uk/fenton-house

13 **Frogmore House**
Home Park, Windsor SL4 1NJ
Open to public: On limited dates, see website for full details
Once a royal retreat, Frogmore is 1.6 kilometres/1 mile from Windsor Castle. It is no longer occupied, but is still used by the royal family for private entertaining. The gardens, which include a lake, were first laid out for Queen Charlotte in the 1790s. Visitors can also enjoy views of Queen Victoria's tea house.
Further information: www.royalcollection.org.uk/visit/frogmorehouse

14 **Fulham Palace**
Bishop's Avenue, London SW6 6EA
Open to public: Gardens every day
The former home of the bishops of London, this is an ancient site and once contained a famous collection of plants developed by Bishop Henry Compton (1623–1713). The surviving garden is mainly nineteenth-century, but it contains a holm oak (*Quercus ilex*) thought to be 450 years old.
Further information: www.fulhampalace.org

15 **Garden Museum**
Lambeth Palace Road, London SE1 7LB
Open to public: All year, apart from Christmas period, see website for full details
The museum's garden was designed in 1980 by Lady Salisbury and forms part of the former churchyard of St Mary-at-Lambeth. The graves of the plant hunters John Tradescant the Elder and his son John are here, as is the tomb of Captain William Bligh, of HMS *Bounty* fame.
Further information:
www.gardenmuseum.org.uk

16 **Geffrye Museum**
136 Kingsland Road, London E2 8EA
Open to public: Period gardens open April to November, Tuesday to Sunday
The period gardens show how domestic gardens have changed over the past four centuries, using evidence garnered from maps, diaries, planting lists, drawings and garden plans. The design for the Tudor Knot Garden, for example, was taken from a motif on an oak cupboard in the museum's 1630 Hall.
Further information:
www.geffrye-museum.org.uk

17 **Gibbon's Rent**
Between Magdalen Street and Holyrood Street, London SE1
Open to public: Every day, year-round
This community garden, designed by award-winning British garden designer Sarah Eberle and Australian architect Andrew Burns, has transformed a dingy alleyway in Bermondsey into a green public space, where local residents can bring their own pots and plants.
Further information:
www.london-se1.co.uk/places/gibbons-rents

18 **The Green Dock**
Thames Barrier Park, North Woolwich Road, London E16 2HP
Open to public: Every day from 7 a.m. to dusk
Often called the Thames Barrier Park, The Green Dock was designed by French landscape architects Alain Provost and Alain Cousseran, working with British architects Patel Taylor. The undulating yew hedges, between 6-m/20-ft 'walls' of *Lonicera nitida* 'Maigrün', make it one of London's most distinctive gardens.
Further information: www.london.gov.uk/priorities/housing-land/land-assets/thames-barrier-park

19 **Green Park**
London SW1A 2BJ
Open to public: Every day, year-round
The smallest of London's eight royal parks, Green Park nonetheless covers 16 hectares/40 acres. It is mainly grass and trees, and a popular site for picnics. There are two war memorials: one commemorates the Canadians who fought with the British in two world wars, while the other is the Bomber Command memorial.
Further information:
www.royalparks.org.uk/parks/green-park

20 **Ham House**
Ham Street, Ham TW10 7RS
Open to public: Gardens almost year-round, see website for full details
The fascinating garden at Ham House, with its formal box parterres, is one of the few grand, seventeenth-century gardens to survive intact. The orangery is the oldest in the UK, and the National Trust, which owns the property, offers free garden tours, which include the kitchen garden.
Further information:
www.nationaltrust.org.uk/ham-house

21 **The Hill Garden and Pergola**
Entrance from North End Way or Inverforth Close, London NW3 7EX
Open to public: Every day, 8.30 a.m. until dusk
The 244-m/800-ft pergola was designed by architect Thomas Mawson for Lord Leverhulme, who bought the property, now called Inverforth House, in 1904. It was designed to be the setting for extravagant parties as well as offering views of the gardens, Hampstead Heath and Harrow Church.
Further information:
www.opensquares.org/detail/hill.html

22 **Holland Park**
Ilchester Place, London W8 6LU
Open to public: Every day, 7.30 a.m. until 30 minutes before dusk
Holland Park has the feel of a local park with the look of a grand garden. Formerly a Jacobean estate, it now hosts the Opera Holland Park season on the terrace of Holland House (the park's peacocks like to join in the arias). The Kyoto Japanese Garden was built in 1991, a gift from the Kyoto Chamber of Commerce.
Further information: www.rbkc.gov.uk/leisureandlibraries/parksandgardens/yourlocalpark/hollandpark.aspx

23 The Holme Inner Circle
Regent's Park, London NW1 4NT
Open to public: Yes, under the National Gardens
Scheme
The vast expanses of Regent's Park include
several large properties – such as London Zoo.
The Holme is a 1.6-hectare/4-acre garden around
a house built by Decimus Burton, original
architect of the zoo. Plantaholics will enjoy the
wide choice of plants, and there is a rock garden
with a stream and waterfall.
Further information: www.ngs.org.uk

24 Hyde Park
London W2 2UH
Open to public: Every day, 5 a.m. to midnight
A royal park since the days of Henry VIII, who
acquired it from the monks of Westminster
Abbey, Hyde Park covers 142 hectares/350 acres
and includes Speaker's Corner, the Princess Diana
Memorial Fountain and the Serpentine, created in
the 1730s and designed to look like a natural lake.
Further information:
www.royalparks.org.uk/parks/hyde-park

25 Isabella Plantation
Richmond Park (enter by Kingston Gate or
Ham Gate) KT2 7NA
Open to public: Every day, see website for details
Part of Richmond Park, the Isabella Plantation
as it is today was created in the 1950s and 1960s,
and is designed to provide year-round interest,
making it a good garden to visit in winter or
early spring. It houses the National Collection of
Kurume azaleas, introduced to the UK by plant
hunter Ernest Wilson in the 1920s.
Further information: www.royalparks.org.uk/
parks/richmond-park/richmond-park-attractions/
isabella-plantation

26 Kensington Gardens
Entrance from Kensington Road or Bayswater
Road, London W2 2UH
Open to public: Every day, year-round
Kensington Gardens surround Kensington Palace,
former home of Princess Diana, and include the
Princess Diana Memorial Playground. A new
allotment garden offers advice on veg growing,
while the statue of Peter Pan commemorates
J.M. Barrie's famous children's stories, inspired
by the gardens.
Further information: www.royalparks.org.uk/
parks/kensington-gardens

27 Kenwood House
Hampstead Lane, London NW3 7JR
Open to public: Every day, see website for
full details especially at Christmas and Easter
This was the home of Lord Mansfield and his
great niece, Dido Belle, now the subject of a
movie. The gardens were designed in the English
Landscape style by Humphry Repton at the end of
the eighteenth century, and the ancient woodland
– more than a third of the 45 hectares/112 acres –
is a Site of Special Scientific Interest.
Further information: www.english-heritage.org.
uk/daysout/properties/kenwood

28 Lambeth Palace
Lambeth Palace Road, London SE1 7JU
Open to public: Yes, for charitable events and
for the National Gardens Scheme
The second-largest private garden in London
(only Buckingham Palace is bigger) and the
oldest continuously cultivated garden in London,
the garden at Lambeth Palace dates from the
twelfth century. Its monastic history inspired
the Chapel Garden, which is planted with herbs,
and there is also an eighteenth-century rotunda.
Further information:
www.archbishopofcanterbury.org/pages/
visit-the-lambeth-palace-gardens-.html

29 London Wetlands Centre
Queen Elizabeth's Walk, London SW13 9WT
Open to public: Every day except Christmas Day
Lakes, ponds and gardens attract a huge range of
wading and other birds to this reserve in the pretty
Thames-side village of Barnes, ten minutes from
Hammersmith. Avocets are among the spring
visitors, while bitterns, one of the rarest breeding
birds in the UK, can be seen in autumn and winter.
Further information: www.wwt.org.uk/
wetland-centres/london

30 The Midnight Apothecary
The Brunel Museum, Railway Avenue,
London SE16 4LF
Open to public: At weekends in summer and
for seasonal events
When gardener Lottie Muir began to develop the
community plot at The Brunel Museum, she gave
out seeds to neighbours so they could grow their own
vegetables. Now she also dispenses cocktails, such
as gin lavender fizz or raspberry martini, using herbs
and produce from the garden, at her pop-up bar.
Further information:
www.thecocktailgardener.co.uk

31 Nomura International plc
1 Angel Lane, London EC4R 3AB
Open to public: Yes, under the Open Squares
Scheme
A vast, sixth-floor roof terrace – the size of eight
tennis courts – provides staff and clients with a
place to eat al fresco during the summer months
while enjoying the gardens and the views of
London's skyline. The kitchen garden, which
measures 17 m × 6 m/56 ft × 20 ft, is managed
voluntarily by the switchboard team.
Further information:
www.opensquares.org/detail/Nomura.html

32 Osterley Park
Jersey Road, Isleworth TW7 4RB
Open to public: Yes, see website for full details
An enchanting mix of formal gardens, lake
and wildflower meadow. Restoration of the
formal gardens from overgrown wilderness to
eighteenth-century grandeur has been aided by
the discovery of documents in America showing
lists of plants ordered for Osterley in 1788.
Further information:
www.nationaltrust.org.uk/osterley-park

33 Paddock Allotments and Leisure Gardens
51 Heath Drive, London SW20 9BE
Open to public: Yes, under the National
Gardens Scheme
A chance to wander round a typical London
allotment, with more than 150 plots, which vary
in character from traditional cottage-garden styles
to straightforward veg beds. Allotment holders
grow a vast range of flowers, fruit and vegetables,
and produce is on sale during the open day.
Further information: www.ngs.org.uk

34 Phoenix Community Garden
21 Stacey Street, London WC2H 8DG
Open to public: Every day until dusk, unless
maintenance work is in progress. The garden
entrance is in St Giles Passage (signposted from
Shaftesbury Avenue and Charing Cross Road)
This community garden was created by local
volunteers in 1984 on the site of a former car
park. There is only a thin layer of soil over
rubble, but the garden is never watered – the
choice of drought-tolerant plants means it can
rely on natural rainfall. Poppies, echiums,
abelia, euphorbia and grevillea are among the
tough performers.
Further information: www.thephoenixgarden.org

35 Postman's Park
St Martin's Le Grand, London EC1A 4AS
Open to public: Every day, 8 a.m. to 7 p.m.
or dusk, whichever is earlier
The park got its name from its popularity as
a lunchtime destination for workers from the
nearby Old Post Office. Created from the
churchyards of St Leonard, Foster Lane and
St Botolph, Aldersgate as well as the graveyard
of Christ Church, Newgate Street, it was laid out
as a public garden in 1880.
Further information: www.cityoflondon.gov.uk/
things-to-do/green-spaces/city-gardens/visitor-
information/Pages/Postman's-Park.aspx

36 Ranelagh Gardens
Royal Hospital Chelsea, Royal Hospital Road,
London SW3 4SR
Open to public: Yes, see website for full details
Now used for RHS Chelsea Flower Show, it is
difficult to remember that Ranelagh Gardens,
the pleasant wooded area on the east of the
showground, was once a rather raffish venue,
famous for its masquerades. Today, it is the
site of some of the smaller show gardens,
and a very pleasant place to have a picnic.
Further information:
www.chelsea-pensioners.co.uk

37 Red House
Red House Lane, Bexleyheath DA6 8JF
Open to public: Yes, see website for full details
Red House is an early and hugely influential
example of Arts and Crafts architecture. It was
built in 1859 for William Morris, who dreamed
of it becoming a 'Palace of Art' amid the orchards
of what was then Kent. There is still an orchard
in the garden, as well as red brick paths and
climbing roses.
Further information:
www.nationaltrust.org.uk/red-house

38 RHS Garden Wisley
Woking GU23 6QB
Open to public: Every day, see website for details
Being a garden for all seasons, Wisley offers
something for every gardener, whether it is
expert advice, a wonderful plant centre or a huge
range of individual growing areas, including
glasshouses, a rock garden, a vegetable garden,
traditional herbaceous borders, an alpine house
and an extensive orchard.
Further information: www.rhs.org.uk/Gardens/
Wisley/Plan-your-visit

39 Richmond Park
Richmond TW10 5HS (postcode for sat-nav
guidance)
Open to public: Every day, see website for full
details
Richmond is the largest of London's royal parks,
and the largest Site of Special Scientific Interest
in the capital. Its ancient oaks support a vast
range of fungi and invertebrates, including
more than 1,000 species of beetle. Once a royal
hunting ground, there have been red and fallow
deer in the park since 1529.
Further information:
www.royalparks.org.uk/parks/richmond-park

40 The River Cafe Garden
Thames Wharf, Rainville Rd, London W6 9HA
Open to public: Yes, if you are dining at the
restaurant
The garden is too small to produce all the
vegetables for the restaurant, but it symbolizes
the passion of owners Rose Gray and Ruth Rogers
for fresh produce, and it provides an attractive
al fresco dining area. All the planting is in
containers that can be moved around according
to what is in season and looking good.
Further information: www.rivercafe.co.uk

41 Royal Botanic Gardens
Kew TW9 3AB
Open to public: Every day, see website for
full details
You need at least a day to do justice to Kew
Gardens. This world-famous site is huge –
120 hectares/300 acres – and includes historic
glasshouses, magnificent trees, a botanical art
gallery and royal retreats. It is a living library, set
in a beautiful landscape that dates back to 1759.
Further information: www.kew.org

42 The Rubens at the Palace
39 Buckingham Palace Road,
London SW1W 0PS
Open to public: Visible from the street
The Living Wall at the Rubens Hotel has an
ecological function as well as being decorative.
It helps to keep the hotel cooler in summer and
warmer in winter, and the plant list includes
a wide variety of native species, and those
recommended by the Royal Horticultural Society
for attracting pollinators.
Further information: www.rubenshotel.com

43 St Dunstan-in-the-East
St Dunstan's Hill, off Lower Thames Street,
London EC3R 8DX
Open to public: Every day, 8 a.m. to 7 p.m.
or dusk, whichever is earlier
St Dunstan's was bombed during the Second
World War, and rather than restore it the Church
of England decided to turn the ruins into a public
garden. Climbers twine around the old walls and
windows, while plants such as *Cytisus battandieri*
and *Drimys winteri* enjoy the sheltered location.
Further information: www.cityoflondon.gov.uk/
things-to-do/green-spaces/city-gardens/visitor-
information/Pages/St-Dunstan-in-the-East.aspx

44 St Paul's, Covent Garden
Bedford Street, London WC2E 9ED
Open to public: Every day
Known as the Actors' Church, St Paul's was
built by Inigo Jones and its Palladian facade is
at the west end of the busy Covent Garden piazza.
At the rear of the church, in complete contrast,
is a churchyard lined with benches – one of the
few places in the area where you can sit in peace
and quiet.
Further information: www.actorschurch.org

45 The Savill Garden
Windsor Great Park, Wick Lane, Englefield
Green, Windsor TW20 0UU (for sat-navs use
postcode, but note that car park is accessible only
from Wick Lane).
Open to public: Every day, 10 a.m. to 4.30 p.m.
First created by Sir Eric Savill in the 1930s, this
is one of the UK's finest ornamental gardens. The
latest addition is the Rose Garden, designed by
Andrew Wilson and opened by the queen in 2010.
Visitors can wander around the spiralling rose beds
and enjoy the perfume from a raised walkway.
Further information: www.theroyallandscape.
co.uk/gardens-and-landscape/the-savill-garden

46 Syon Park
Brentford TW8 8JF
Open to public: Every day from mid-March
to the end of October
The park at Syon, London home of the dukes
of Northumberland, was designed by Lancelot
'Capability' Brown in 1760. Charles Fowler's
Great Conservatory, completed in 1827, was
the first of its kind to be built of metal and glass.
It is a popular film location for costume dramas.
Further information: www.syonpark.co.uk

Major garden events

Chelsea Fringe
Various venues across London
Open to public: Yes, see website for full details
The Chelsea Fringe is an alternative garden
festival that coincides with RHS Chelsea Flower
Show and runs from the middle of May to the
beginning of June. The brainchild of landscape
critic Tim Richardson, it includes gardens,
installations and community projects among
its 250-plus events.
Further information: www.chelseafringe.com

Open House
Various venues across London
Open to public: Yes, see website for full details
Usually held on the third weekend of September,
this provides a wonderful opportunity to nose
around some of London's most impressive
buildings, and the grounds and gardens that
surround them. Participants include the Foreign
Office, St Mary Axe (aka The Gherkin) and the
Bank of England. Open House London produces
a guide, which is also available from museums
and galleries.
Further information:
www.openhouselondon.org.uk

Open Squares
Various venues across London
Open to public: Yes
The garden equivalent of Open House, Open
Squares showcases more than 200 gardens each
year on the second weekend in June. It includes
not only many of London's garden squares but
also private and community gardens. There are
schools, hotels, offices and even a convent.
Further information: www.opensquares.org

Royal Horticultural Society London shows
RHS Lindley Hall, London SW1P 2QW
and
RHS Lawrence Hall, London SW1P 2QD
Open to public: Yes
You need to book well in advance for RHS
Chelsea Flower Show, but at the smaller London
shows you can usually turn up on the day. The
shows have a seasonal focus, and include spring
bulbs, alpines, roses and autumn colour, with
some of the best nurseries selling their plants.
Further information: www.rhs.org.uk/shows-
events/rhs-london-shows

Acknowledgments

First, an apology to my dog Rufus, and to my cats
Mario and Luigi, who were not impressed by my
frequent absences while I was researching this
book. I'd like to thank my dog-walking friends
Wendy Hazelwood and Beverly Morgan-Davies
for taking Rufus out while I was busy. More
thanks go to my friends Joanna Blythman and
Penny Fox for their moral support, and to Helen
Griffin and Joanna Chisholm at Frances Lincoln
for their help and advice. *VS*

Marianne would like to thank all the garden
owners and designers who have generously
opened their garden gates for her. Thanks to
Helen Griffin, Glenn Howard and the editorial
team at Frances Lincoln. *MM*

Hugo would like to thank HRH The Prince of
Wales, 10 Downing Street, The US Ambassador,
The Royal Historic Palaces, English Heritage
and all the owners of these magnificent gardens
for their generosity and support in achieving
this book. He would also like to extend a special
thanks to Victoria Summerley and, at Frances
Lincoln, Helen Griffin and Glenn Howard, as
well as his collaborator Marianne Majerus. *HRT*